TRUST-BUILDING

AN EXPERIENTIAL APPROACH

Pauline Napier and
Michelle Napier-Dunnings

authorHOUSE®

AuthorHouse™
1663 Liberty Drive, Suite 200
Bloomington, IN 47403
www.authorhouse.com
Phone: 1-800-839-8640

First published by AuthorHouse 12/12/2007

ISBN: 978-1-4343-4166-2 (sc)

Printed in the United States of America
Bloomington, Indiana

This book is printed on acid-free paper.

TRUST

Yet the development of personality means more than just the fear of hatching forth monsters, or of isolation. It also means fidelity to the law of one's own being.

For the word "fidelity" I should prefer, in this context, the Greek word used in the New Testament, πίστις, which is erroneously translated "faith." It really means "trust," "trustful loyalty."

(C.G. Jung. *Collected Works. Vol. 17*, p. 173)

To Fr. Bill Fay,
For years
of
Trustful Loyalty.
Pauline & Michelle

TABLE OF CONTENTS

SECTION ONE:
INTRODUCTION

CHAPTER I
ENGAGING IN THIS WORKBOOK

Engaging in this Workbook
A Suggested Process

This book is designed to engage readers in an interactive process of building a definition of trust, performing exercises designed to elicit experiences of trust, and encouraging the telling of stories that illustrate trust.

Each chapter has three sections:

1. A theoretical discussion based on Carl Gustav Jung's Collected Works (C.W.)
2. An exercise created to put that theory into an experience
3. A story illustrating the concepts from the authors' personal journeys

The reason you were drawn to this workbook will more than likely determine how you want to use it:

- If you start with the <u>theoretical explanations</u>, you may want to hear the basis of our thinking first. What is the main idea in each chapter and what research supports this idea?
- If you are an <u>experiential learner</u>, you may wish to begin each chapter by working through the exercise. This will allow you to process the theory through your personal point of view and life experiences.
- If <u>stories</u> help you "see" the ideas or if you are mainly intrigued with the mother-daughter relationship, these can be read first.

You will hear the movement and interconnection of our voices in each section:

- Pauline wrote the theoretical explanations.
  - To read more about C.G. Jung, we suggest starting with <u>Memories, Dreams, Reflections</u>. (Jung. 1961)
  - As you read, questions will arise that are specifically yours. Follow that energy, and see the Appendix for additional references and information.

- Michelle designed the experiences.
  - Review the "Activity Form" to see what is needed for each experience.
  - Proceed with the experience itself. Each experience is described in steps and with the expectation that the reader will do each step in sequence. (If you are a facilitator of a group, we would suggest that you do the experience first on your own.)

- The Ma & Me Stories were written together.
  - They were chosen to reflect the theme of each chapter. Both of us are storytellers who love to follow the energy in a workshop, even if it takes us "on a tangent!"
  - They are also shared here to give a further glimpse into the world of Pauline and Michelle as both colleagues and a mother-daughter duo. The mere fact that mother and daughter took this walk together impacted people in our workshops.

Trust is a "firm belief or confidence in the honesty, integrity, reliability, justice, etc. of another person or thing; faith; reliance."

(*Webster's Dictionary.* 1966, p.1,565)

WHAT IS YOUR DEFINITION OF TRUST?

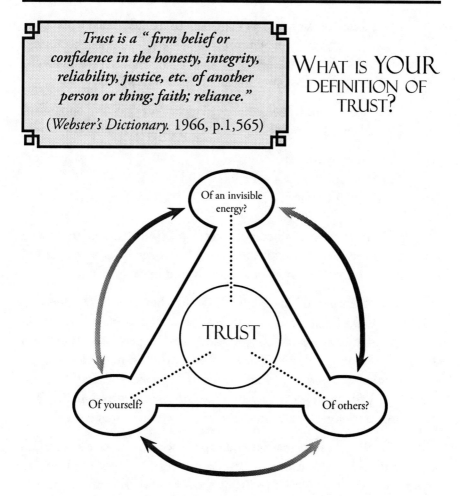

As you move through this interactive collection of ideas, experiences, and stories, build your own personal definition of trust. Sometimes you may find it by looking at what you do *not* trust. Sometimes it will be a person or thing that you have taken for granted. Sometimes your trust is there with very little conscious awareness ~ you may have a trust that you assume everyone has; however, by looking more closely, you realize that this is not true for everyone. The ideas, experiences, and stories in this guide were designed for you to explore the concept of trust and then to build your own understanding and practices that will help you continue to strengthen the trust you currently have for yourself, an invisible energy, and others. (Our term *invisible energy* refers to an autonomous kinetic vigor ~ a force beyond human visibility with a will of its own.)

7

(Jung's view of the nature of man suggests that the individual is born whole ~ not perfect.) His or her entire life is searching for, and contributing to, the wholeness that he or she is. This search affects and establishes the way in which we live in community and in the entire world.

We, the authors, have attempted to explore the development of the individual and this search for wholeness through the challenges of:

1) trusting oneself,
2) trusting an invisible energy, and
3) trusting others.

Transforming conflict becomes a possibility when the above criteria are brought to consciousness. As self-knowledge emerges, action steps toward relatedness may be creatively and humanely revealed.

As mentioned in Pauline's short biography (Appendix), McKenzie Oaks Films produced a conversation between us. Together, we discussed the theories of C.G. Jung and shared experiential techniques designed to embody those theories. The workshop referred to in the film "Human Strength: An Experience of Trust & The Transcendent Function" was given to a group of health care professionals. The content of this workbook follows the basic agenda of that workshop.

Finally, the information and experiences in the following pages may be used by the reader in private or with any group willing to explore self-knowledge as a basis for growth ~ whether the nature of that group be economic, educational, communal, or cultural.

ENTERING INTO THE PROCESS
Activity Form

Purpose
To explore where your roots of trust reside, and to tap those roots for the hope and energy needed in trust-building.

Materials needed
- Plain paper
- Colored pencils or crayons
- Music (optional)

Space needed
A comfortable, safe place to draw and reflect.

Number of people
Alone.

Time necessary

STEP ONE	10 minutes
STEP TWO	15-20 minutes
STEP THREE	20 minutes
STEP FOUR	10 minutes
STEP FIVE	20-30 minutes

Desired outcomes
1. To identify consciously a safe childhood place and the person, animal, object, and/or presence that was there with you
2. To learn the steps for asking your trustful image for support
3. To look at how our earlier experiences can help us rediscover and build trust

ENTERING INTO THE PROCESS
Experience

STEP ONE

Allow your mind to wander back to a place and time before you were fifteen years old (before conventions permitted you to travel on your own).

Pick one age.

Now answer the following questions about the world in which you lived at that age:

- What did your environment look like – the geographical terrain?
- What buildings inhabited your world (home, church, school, community center, etc.)?
- Who were the important people?
- What did you love to do?
- What were you good at doing?
- What was the general feeling of being in that world (exciting, peaceful, worrisome, etc.)?

STEP TWO

After briefly answering these questions, draw a "map" of your world at that age. Do not worry about your artistic ability. Feel free to use stick people and two-dimensional buildings. Also, things do not have to be drawn to size – a very important activity or person may take up a large part of your "map."

Take as much time as possible to draw, use lots of color, and feel free to have music playing in the background.

STEP THREE

Turn the "map" over and answer the question: "Did I feel safe anywhere in this map and, if so, **who or what was there with me, watching over me and caring for me?**"

> Note: Children seek out places, people, or fantasies that give them a sense of security. If your childhood map holds much that was unsafe, try to find what "spot" you loved to be in the most and what person, animal, object, or imaginary entity shared that experience with you.

Immediately draw or write a few sentences about that image ~ the person, animal, object, and/or presence that was there with you, watching over you, and caring for you in that safe place.

Give your image a name and write it down.

STEP FOUR

1. Close your eyes and settle into a comfortable position.
2. Breathe deeply ~ in through your nose, focusing on the tip of your nose (repeat five times).
3. After each breath, repeat the name of your image.
4. Feel the trust of that image in this present moment ~ notice where that trust resides in your body. Trust that you are being cared for right now.

STEP FIVE

Bring that trusting energy into your world.

When you open your eyes, you may wish to:

*   add to your image picture,
*   write how you are feeling, and/or
*   find an object or picture that can be placed in your space today to remind you of this trustful energy.

Keep this trustful image close.

QUESTIONS FOR REFLECTION

You are basically looking for a way to re-enter a trusting place and time. And in that place and time, to reacquaint yourself with the trusting entity that was there with you.

There are many questions you can ask. When did you first connect with that image? How did it come into your life? How did it accompany you throughout childhood?
Allow the questions here to guide you as you explore the meaning of this image and its relationship to you.

As we reflect on this experience, it is important to realize that the world that was drawn in your "map" may not be one that you think of much; yet, it lies very close to the surface of your consciousness. The experiences in that world affect your daily actions. Furthermore, your trustful image can help guide you through this trust-building journey.

WORKING TOGETHER
Ma & Me Story

Pauline, Ma (*mah*), and I have been working together professionally since 1995. From that point till now, she and I have been companions on a professional and personal journey.

It has been extraordinary.

The first time we presented in a corporate setting we thought we might not mention that we were related. Maybe it would be uncomfortable and "unprofessional" for the group to know that we were mother and daughter. Perhaps they would think it so strange that our message would be overshadowed. We knew there were lots of written and assumed rules around nepotism in the workplace. But, there were no rules of conduct for a mother-daughter consulting team! We decided to be as subtle as possible, refer to each other as Pauline and Michelle, and not address the relationship issue.

Ha!

About halfway through the first workshop, we unexpectedly mentioned our familial connection and everyone in the room laughed! It was so obvious. We look alike, we talk alike, we even sometimes walk alike (note: the theme from The Patty Duke Show!) and the group said there was no way to hide that we were related.

So after that, I usually called her "Ma" and she did not refrain from giving me "a parental evil eye" when correcting my actions (much as she had when I was a child). Groups found this fascinating. They were very responsive to the material we presented and always intrigued with our relationship ~ the ability to respect each other's perspective, the playful bantering when we disagreed, the management of tension between us when things got more intense, and the overt celebration of each other's unique gifts. They experienced a "public relationship of trust" between two women, two professionals, who happened to be mother and daughter.

It is important to realize that these years of working together have not been "easy" points in either of our lives. Pauline was moving into the fourth quarter of her life, still very much engaged in her own private practice, her husband, five children and twelve grandchildren's lives, and the care of her aging mother. I was approaching mid-life. I had a successful career, a wonderful family, and an extended network of people who truly loved me. However, I was beginning to feel less sure of myself rather than more so.

Ironically (or typically, as life so often demonstrates), we were being offered opportunities to teach others how to trust themselves ~ to develop an awareness of the gifts and talents they had and to strategize how to use those for purposeful work. As we responded to these opportunities, we found how common it was for accomplished professionals, in the second half of life, to struggle with trusting themselves and those around them. People could intellectually discuss trust in the workplace and the importance of working in diverse teams of people; *but* not far below the surface, the level of distrust of the world and themselves was palpable. The talk in the group stayed quite superficial, but the talk in one-on-one coaching sessions did not!

We repeatedly saw successful people in mid-life and those well into the second half, losing a sense of trust in others and themselves. No matter how brilliantly the world defined their offerings and level of accomplishments, the distrust was there.

Not only that, but because of their positions, it was even more difficult to acknowledge and address these feelings of mistrust. Speaking for myself, I had worked hard to get where I was. As a consultant, people expected me to be sure of my answers and myself. So when the "wicked devil of doubt" began dropping in, I kept "her" hidden from my colleagues and sometimes from me!

I found myself on a personal journey; teaching what I needed to learn! Pauline was teaching what she had lived and was obliged to give

back. We agreed then and agree now that the strength to trust is an ⌐ ✓
intellectual, emotional, physical, and spiritual phenomenon.

For example, in the beginning of Chapter V, Pauline discusses the concept of
conflict within the human development framework of Carl Jung's theories.
His writings confirmed and expanded upon her lifelong intellectual and
intuitive knowledge. In that same chapter, I describe an experience of
integrating the labyrinth walk into the process of transcending conflict.
When I first built a labyrinth ~ a physical and spiritual activity for me ~
I began both to understand it and to "gnow" it (Lonegren. 2001, p.11).
The word "gnow" comes from "gnosis" and the prefix "gno," meaning to
know. The American Heritage Dictionary defines gnosis as an "intuitive
apprehension of spiritual truths, an esoteric form of knowledge sought by
the Gnostics." (American Heritage Dictionary. 1975, p.563)

Each of us can truly "gnow" trust only through our individual
personality, in relation to our personal experiences, and by involving
our whole selves. The "gnowing" comes when all of our senses, our
thoughts and our feelings embrace the moment ~ an experience which
eludes us when we try too hard to "get it." Yet that "getting it" feeling
is always right there if we can learn to listen.

Clearly, we are not advocating that all of you create a business
relationship with one of your parents in order to implement the ideas
in this book! We are advocating a conscious practice of building trust
so that you may experience a personal and professional life that has
energy and meaning.

Pauline and I have talked for long and seemingly endless hours about
possibilities in the world ~ both the world we see and can touch, and the
world of the imagination. I have had a number of excellent professional
coaches. However, from that first time we presented a corporate workshop
together, Ma has been my mentor and (as always) one of my biggest
cheerleaders. She trusted that my gifts and ideas were powerful and that I
needed encouragement for stepping up and sharing them with the world.
I am grateful to the invisible energy for the gifts I was given at birth and for
the motivating challenges that have appeared on this journey.

And I am profoundly grateful for Ma ~ for her heroic modeling behavior
and her undeniable trust in me.

CHAPTER II
WHY "TRUST-BUILDING?"

WHY "TRUST-BUILDING?"
The Importance of this Work

In a worldview of death and destruction, misery and depression, sadness and grief; violence and intolerance reign. Is there an antidote to compensate for the dissolution of humanity? Has the human race, for the necessity of self-preservation, become addicted to the blocking of fear and pain at any cost?

One major course for blocking fear and pain is through the use of both legal and illegal drugs. In U.S. culture (perhaps throughout the world), the use of drugs to immunize fear and pain is rampant. (Napier. 2003)

Stanton Peele in his seminal in-depth study of addiction concludes that the cure for addiction rests not in the use of drugs but in the capacity to experience joy and competence. He defines joy as "the capacity to take pleasure in the people, activities and the things that are available to us." For Peele, competence is "the ability to master relevant parts of the environment and the confidence that our actions make a difference for ourselves and others." Peele concludes that "preparing people better to achieve joy and competence offers us our only substantial chance at affecting the incidence of addiction. It is certainly not a modest goal: Some might call it utopian or quixotic. Yet to the extent that our addiction theories avoid this realization . . . we will only obfuscate and exacerbate the addictive tendencies of our society." (Peele. 1985, p.157)

While I am in agreement with Peele's insight for the dire need to crack the barriers that block joy and competence, to take pleasure in people or have confidence that one's life can make a difference requires some level of trust.

Without a sense of basic trust, hope is lost. In Erik Erikson's classical research on the "Psychosocial Stages of Life," he proposes eight stages of psychosocial development:

1. First year of life	Trust vs. mistrust	(Hope)
2. Second year	Autonomy vs. doubt	(Will)
3. Third – fifth year	Initiative vs. guilt	(Purpose)
4. Sixth year – puberty	Industry vs. inferiority	(Competence)
5. Adolescence	Identity vs. confusion	(Fidelity)
6. Early adulthood	Intimacy vs. isolation	(Love)
7. Middle adulthood	Generativity vs. self-absorption	(Care)
8. The aging years	Integrity vs. despair	(Wisdom)

(Hilgard, Atkinson, Atkinson. 1979, p.95)

Erikson has found that in the very first year of life, in infancy, "Trust versus Mistrust" is formed. In his view, the development of trust is the foundational stage for the development of human interaction. He puts forth the idea that competence emerges during the fourth stage of development, from the sixth year of life to puberty. The infant cannot address the problematic issue of trust. Nor can the adolescent rectify the loss of basic trust. It is the vital task of each *adult* to strengthen consciously one's self for the self-knowledge of "Trust."

It seems clear that the tremendously complex issue of "Trust" must have a voice. Carl Jung poses the notion that trust was the key to the development of a humane relationship within and between cultures. His theory of the nature of man and the importance of the "second half of life" provides a hope that an individual can and must find the strength to examine the meaning and purpose of life. This process is in its human infancy. Without basic trust, all else pales.

While the issue of trust permeates our every living moment, like beauty, it is elusive, context-bound and relegated to philosophers. We must concretize trust. How does one approach an ephemeral entity? Very carefully, and with an open-minded tolerance that does not immediately reject the effort with criticism of its simplicity and non-scholarly proof of its assumptions.

Our presentation in this book is one step in an attempt to approach trust in an empirical manner. (We, the advocates of the *N B* following approach, believe that without trust there can be no hope,) no purpose, no meaning to humane life. This view suggests, as Carl Jung has, that if the individual takes up the task of self-knowledge, the world has the possibility to humanize. If the individual passes this task on to an institution, an ideology, or a charismatic leader, freedom of the individual as well as society is destroyed.

In the second half of life, we need to be taught to listen to our own natures (Jung. C.W. Vol.17, p.62) ~ to release that part of ourselves for life to continue into late years, those gifted years of new growth. Man endures a meaningless life when the difficult but rewarding journey for self-knowledge, i.e., analyzing himself or herself, has been buried under the supremacy of the masses. The word analysis stems from the Greek "analusis," which means "a releasing." Repressing this nature " . . . has the apparent advantage of clearing the conscious mind of worry . . . however it radiates into the environment . . . In this way neurotic states are often passed on from generation to generation . . ." (Jung. C.W. Vol.17, p.78)

We, of the wisdom years, leave to the next generation our unlived search for self-knowledge. We leave the image of extended life as self-absorption and despair. We leave the notion that the energy, struggles, and successes experienced in the first half of life are meaningless.

In the television program *Face to Face*, Jung's interviewer, John Freeman, concluded by saying:

> "And this leads me to the last question that I want to ask you. As the world becomes more technically efficient it seems increasingly necessary for people to behave communally and collectively. Now do you think it possible that the highest development of man may be to submerge his own individuality in a kind of collective consciousness?"

Jung responded:

> "That's hardly possible. I think there will be a reaction. A reaction will set in against this communal dissociation.

You know, man doesn't stand forever his nullification. Once there will be a reaction, and I see it setting in. You know when I think of my patients, they all seek their own existence against that complete atomization into nothingness, or into meaninglessness. Man cannot stand a meaningless life."

(Jung. *Face to Face,* 1959)

Our elementary approach to this vast, complex enigma requires an audience of adults in the second half of life - those persons who have survived Erikson's first six stages of psychosocial development and have reached a critical seventh stage of middle adulthood, where concern for family, society, and future generations come up against self-absorption. If one takes the path of care and generativity, we may in the eighth stage, the aging years, find wisdom and integrity, versus despair.

EXPANDING THE CHILDHOOD MAP
Activity Form

Purpose
To explore a few experiences, thus far in your life, of joy and competency and their relation to the feeling of trust.

Materials needed
- Plain paper
- Colored pencils or crayons
- Music (optional)

Space needed
A comfortable, safe place to draw and reflect.

Number of people
Step One thru Step Five ~ Alone.
Additional ideas ~ Alone or with a trusted friend.

Time necessary

STEP ONE	10 minutes
STEP TWO	15-20 minutes
STEP THREE	20 minutes
STEP FOUR	30 minutes
STEP FIVE	20-30 minutes
Additional Ideas	30-60 minutes

Desired outcomes
1. To identify areas of joy and competence throughout your life
2. To look for patterns in these areas
3. To consider the relationship of joy and competence to the feeling of trust

Expanding the Childhood Map
Experience

STEP ONE

Go back to the childhood map created in Chapter I.
Pick a number between five and nine.
Add that number to the age in the Chapter I map.

Briefly respond again to the questions below, now for this second age:

- What did your environment look like ~ the geographical terrain?
- What buildings inhabited your world (home, church, school, community center, etc.)?
- Who were the important people?
- What did you love to do?
- What were you good at doing?
- What was the general feeling of being in that world (exciting, peaceful, worrisome, etc.)?

STEP TWO

Again draw a "map" of this age's world.

> Remember: Do not worry about your artistic ability. Feel free to use stick people and two-dimensional buildings. Things do not have to be drawn to size ~ a very important activity or person may take up a large part of your "map."
>
> Take as much time as possible to draw, use lots of color, and feel free to have music playing in the background.

STEP THREE

Repeat Step One & Step Two ~ you will end up with three maps at various intervals of your life (for example, ten, seventeen, and twenty-four years old).

STEP FOUR

Reflect on the consistencies from one childhood map to another:

- What is similar in the maps?
- What personal talents and skills show up over and over in each picture?
- How did you acquire those talents and skills? Did you learn them or were you born with them? (Ex: I could always sing. A neighbor taught me how to play the guitar.)
- How are the activities, people, and places that brought you joy similar to each other?

STEP FIVE

Make a list of your joys and competencies.
This list can be referred to in later experiences (Chapter III and IV).

- Look around you today ~ Are any of the ingredients in that list "living" in your "map" today?
- Is it possible to nurture a couple of "seeds of joy and competency" from this list in your world today?

IDEAS FOR REFLECTION

It is possible that you will not initially recognize some of your talents and skills. So often when we are naturally good at something and it comes easily to us, we do not identify it as a talent. We think everyone can do that!

> You may wish to share one or more of the maps with a trusted friend. Basically, describe the world in the map and then ask them to answer the question "Do you see talents and skills in this picture?" And try to just listen! Someone else may see your natural gifts more easily

than you do because s/he is different than you, his/her experiences are different, and s/he is looking at these maps as an observer, not a participant. When s/he is finished, discuss the relationship to what you both see in the map to your perceptions of strengths and weaknesses at this stage of your life.

Keep these maps with this workbook. They can be referred to as you engage in later experiences (particularly in Chapters III, IV, and V).

If you are energized after making the maps, you may wish to look for additional patterns that have gone into the fabric of your life.

- How are the challenges in those ages similar to the challenges now?
- How did the similar rules impact you?
- Did you carry any of those rules into your adult life?
- Who else at various ages gave you strength and courage?
- What events significantly changed the feeling from one map to another?
- How did the rules in each map's world impact you?
- How did the rules change?

A Youthful Container of Trust
Ma & Me Story

Ma and I talk a great deal about creating a container of trust when we prepare for our workshops. This container holds an atmosphere, a mood, the physical space, and behavioral expectations. The container helps participants to take small risks, to open up a little in order to experience a slightly different idea or process.

The container has boundaries. Pauline is adamant that we not "spill our guts!" She is very private in her approach, actually encouraging secrets to be held. I am more energized when the group has an "aha" that I believe can shift how they function collectively, outside the workshop.

Ma and I agree completely on the combination of content presentation and experiential activities, encouraging participants to understand both intellectually and "in their muscles." However, we struggle over how to process the learning. Ma's focus is individual change and mine is group dynamics. We recognize the value of both and try to find a conscientious balance. We want participants to leave feeling stronger, not publicly exposed. Consequently, in order for Ma and me to trust our work together, we must create this safe container for the group and for ourselves as co-facilitators.

I realize this "container" and the process for creating it was introduced to me as a small child. The backyard of my childhood home was my safe container. It was located in a valley behind our house and connected by a honeysuckled path, running from the basement door to the open area below. The yard itself was a cleared acre, surrounded by woods. A creek flowed along one side of it.

There were two sections to this backyard, divided by a low line of hedges. The back section held our doghouse and a little garden my siblings and I tended. The garden never produced much harvest - maybe a few tiny carrots. Part of the problem was hauling fresh water the long trek from the house to the plot!

In the front section of the yard was a big apple tree with a tree house, a swampy area where wild mint grew, a hill running down to the creek, and a swing set in full view of the upstairs kitchen window. Ma was close to that window when I was alone in the backyard. I loved to swing and sing my little heart out! My voice carried out to the yard, into the woods, and up to the kitchen where I knew Ma was watching and listening with a huge smile in her heart.

Lots of stories came out of that yard - like the time my brother and I were sledding before a friend's birthday party. My hair was in curlers under my hat. I zoomed down the hill toward the creek and couldn't stop. The sled plunged into the creek. My brother ran down and scooped me up, trying not to laugh at the mud in my curlers and my pitiful tears as he carried me up the hill to the house. I was unharmed but hysterical. Needless to say, my hair ended up in a bun for that birthday party!

Another story we all tell involved of one of my cousins who was constantly biting other kids. One day he bit me. I began to cry. Ma came down into the backyard to soothe my crying pain. She asked my cousin, "Do you know how much it hurts when you bite someone?" He looked at her with innocent eyes. "No," he said. "Let me show you," Ma said. My cousin never bit me again.

When I step back and reflect, I see my first introduction to a safe public space. There was no fence to keep others out. Even though crowds of people rarely occupied it, a friend, a relative, and sometimes the neighbor's dog would come over. There were some very basic guidelines and activities that made that space so precious and safe to me.

> There were simple rules like "never leave the yard without telling Mom, and take turns on the swings."

> There was an expectation that everyone would pitch in to care for the yard. It was quite a large space to cut the grass with a hand-pushed mower. The short hedges always

needed trimming and the honeysuckle lining the path from the basement grew faster than any of the children.

There was an understanding that each of us needed the yard for different reasons. It was a sledding and skiing training ground, a climbing and secret hideout place, a view of solace filled with beautiful smells, and a stage for singing to the animals in the woods and to Ma.

The memories of that safe container reconnect me with early experiences of competence and joy.

Those memories and experiences also inform the creation of effective workshop spaces. For instance, workshop participants need to know what the rules are. When people attend our sessions, they are expected to participate actively rather than passively watch. In order to support that expectation, we talk to the group about specific behaviors that will allow everyone to join in comfortably. These behaviors include standing up to stretch during a presentation, getting another cup of coffee at any time, and feeling free to decline to comment even when asked a direct question.

Ma and I also try to care for the physical space. We attend to how the room is arranged, what items add beauty, and the comfort of the set-up (preferably, small groups of tables and chairs). Of course, we have different opinions here too. Pauline would like to do workshops in caves ~ she loves dark and enclosed spaces. I want an open feeling with sunlight and windows. We do our best to adjust to what our clients have to offer while simultaneously making sure each other gets what she needs (if necessary, outside the workshop when it is not available within it).

And finally, we know that individuals come to workshops for very different reasons. Some are told to be there, so their needs are initially polarized from those who have chosen to attend. Like Ma and me, some want to share very few of their personal views and others want to let it all hang out! Some are looking for ideas on how to deal with a problematic co-worker, while some want to move up in their work and need new skills to do so.

The preparation before and at the outset of each workshop directly impacts the day. As co-facilitators, we have consciously looked at our preferences, compromised with each other, and then adjusted to the clients' situations. It is extraordinary to realize that this dance between Ma and me has been going on since I was a little girl.

Everyone does not have the memory of such a backyard and of performing for his/her mom. This experience was a gift that enabled me to create these spaces for others. It also grounded me in my personal understanding of trust. Pauline encouraged me to acknowledge that spaces may become dangerous, that it is important to know whom I can call on for help when that occurs, and that it is possible to incorporate consciously ingredients from my childhood into trust-building experiences in the present.

A few years ago, I was inspired to renew and expand my backyard lessons. I had lived in my current home since 1991. I truly liked the location but did not feel passionately connected to my surroundings. I mowed, trimmed, planted flowers, and harvested a "few scrawny carrots" in my small backyard.

Then I was introduced to labyrinths (see Chapter V). I fell in love with the history and metaphor of the life journey contained in this ancient path. My younger sister insisted I pick a date so she could come and help me build a labyrinth in my backyard. For weeks, I was immersed in the preparations – mapping out the path, ordering a truckload of rocks from a local landscaping company, and having the rocks delivered to the side yard near the street as neighbors drove by and gawked.

At five-thirty in the morning on June 7, 2003, I began setting stakes in the ground and lugging the rocks to the backyard (some impossible to lift even with two people). My husband, uninterested in the endeavor yet supporting me, made delicious chili for all my worker friends. My intrigued neighbors offered refreshments, snacks, equipment, and additional muscle to move the biggest rocks. They learned about labyrinths while confirming their assessment that I was a "little bit different!"

By sunset, the path was built and my sister and I were filthy and exhausted.

What I didn't realize until then was how much I needed that space – where I could journey safely, explore my inner "woods" and look for the energy to step into the outer world with more trust.

My childhood and my adult backyards have taught me a great deal about trust. They have taught me what I need in order to reflect and build trust in myself, how nature and the invisible energy periodically grace those spaces, and how others can enter into that space from different perspectives. (My husband and children are still less than enthusiastic about the labyrinth. It takes up the entire backyard, the sunbathing chair must be balanced between the rocks, and the grass can only be trimmed with an edge trimmer!)

Even though my family does not find walking the path quite as inspiring as I do, not one of them derailed my project. Each understands how important it was for me to build this container. I have learned not to expect them to need the same things I do. And, grace has entered that space more than once. Last Easter, we all had "church" there. All four of us walked the labyrinth and said our prayers for each other, the world, and ourselves. I was in heaven. They were happy for me!

SECTION TWO:
THE THREE TRUSTS

CHAPTER III
TRUSTING ONESELF

TRUSTING ONESELF
Nature of Man ~ Stages of Life ~ Carl Gustav Jung

Carl Jung's view of the nature of man suggests that the individual is born whole, not perfect. And his/her entire life is dedicated to searching for the wholeness that s/he is. This life-long work of relationship to oneself, to an invisible energy, and to others Jung called *individuation*. The notion of the process of individuation gives credence to a life lived fully with all of its joys and sorrows. It brings hope (vs. despair) that regardless of one's inadequacies and life circumstances, whether one is sixteen, sixty, or seventy-five years old, each day will bring together two different aspects of life: those that one is conscious of ~ both about oneself and the world in which one lives; and those aspects which have not yet been revealed. It is a life-giving energy that makes living tomorrow worthwhile.

For me, three major concepts arise about human nature taken from Jung's perspective:

1) The Victim Question,
2) The Need for Trust and Hope, and
3) The Search for Purpose and Meaning.

In Jung's view, one is not stuck forever as the victim of his/her birth, parents, and the societal era in which one is born. The infant brings into the world a multi-generational history that interacts with the concrete worldly relationship to time, place, and those persons who are crucial to the survival of the newborn. But, vital as it is, this is the beginning of one's story. What effect does the complex situation into which one is born have on the child? How does the response that the child makes to that complex situation affect his/her life? In other words, how does human relationship begin? There is no formula to answer these questions since each personal relationship differs, even for siblings born to the same parents and into the same societal era. Rather than seeing this relationship building as an issue to be solved, we can approach this reality as a life-giving, energizing quest for relationship.

(On some level, we are all victims of circumstance. However, to move from a crippling victimization to a trust in oneself requires a relationship with oneself, the life from which we came, and the life into which we will journey.)

Through extensive scientific inquiry, modern thinkers have found some paths to essential human relationship, be they individual or universal. However, it is painfully clear that scientific inquiry, valuable as it is, has led the individual and the world to lean heavily on the capacity for destruction, rather than relationship. Jung believed, as do we, that this transformative process from destruction to relationship must begin with the individual. For it is only the individual, not the institution, who can address the fantasy and mystery of the personality. Without addressing the mysterious way in which life unfolds in a person, the fantastic transformation from destruction to relationship remains elusive. We live in a world of victimization without trust or hope that what one person does or does not do makes a difference. This powerlessness sets the stage for fear and violence to others and to oneself. Where are trust and hope when human scientific discovery, taken to extreme, is the destroyer?

(The human race cannot survive without some basic notion of trust and hope.) If you are reading this sentence and have reached a number of years of life on this earth, somewhere in your personal history you have had an experience of a safe environment where trust and hope reside.

Search for it!

Trust and hope cannot be created in a laboratory. These fundamental structures of a personality originate from stimuli within the human body. It is essential that the individual experience these constructs of trust and hope in order to find purpose and meaning in this earthly life ~ to bear witness to the possibility that an individual can make a difference and to understand that there is an unknown aspect to living that is as factual as the existence of the sun and the moon.

"THE STAGES OF LIFE"

First Half of Life ~ Emphasis on Ego Development

Childhood	Rapid Mental and Physical Growth
Youth	Strengthening of Identity Through External Accomplishments

Second Half of Life ~ Emphasis on Soul Development

Middle Life	While Retaining Ego Consciousness, Wrestling with Problems Concerning the Meaning of Your Life
Old Age	Giving Back to Society and Preparing for Death

(Jung. C.W. Vol. 8, pp.387-403)

A synopsis of Jung's outline above might read:

> In the first half of life,
> **you do for others to help yourself.**
> In the second half of life,
> **you do for yourself to help others.**

Jung refers to the Stages of Life wherein the first half of life must be grounded in the scientific concrete, developing a stable ego (center of consciousness) that can interact with and integrate into the personality's unconscious energy, which is patiently waiting to be heard. A dialogue with the energies from the unconscious may be creatively experienced in the second half of life. In our era of the evolution of man, we can speak of the second half of life. The National Center for Health

Statistics, U.S. Department of Human Services, reports that in 1900 the average life span for a man was 46.3 years; for a woman, it was 48.3 years. In 2002 the average life span rose to 74.6 for a man and 79.9 for a woman. There is a significant number of years unaccounted for in the development of the individual. Medical research has successfully focused on the illnesses of that period, extending the quantity of life. Where is the information for the development of the personality of those persons in the second half of life?

> "We have to educate adults who are no longer willing, like children, to be guided by authority. We have to do with men and women whose way of life is so individual that no counselor, however wise, could prescribe the way that is uniquely right for them. <u>Therefore we have to teach them to listen to their own natures</u> (underlining mine) so that they can understand from within themselves what is happening."

> (Jung. C.W. Vol. 17, p.62)

Jung comments that adults have never been taught about the requirements of life after forty. Where are the books written for the education of the adult personality?

This adult group must be educated as a guide for the next generation. These adults are the ones who have asked the questions of life and who have suffered through the void toward joy and competence, into a place of trustworthiness and wisdom.

In this second half of life, many individuals are confronted with earth-shattering questions of trust, hope, purpose, and meaning. Jung understood that the work required for this questioning is not for children. As he points out, it would rob them of their childhood. These processes are not expected of the adolescent either. In "The Stages of Life" (C.W. Vol. 8), Jung emphasizes the fact that the first half of life must be grounded in the concrete where mental and physical growth occurs and external accomplishments take precedence. During this period, concrete reality develops in a firm and trustful relationship with adults.

During an interview, Colin Powell, the former U.S. Secretary of State, was asked how an ordinary kid rose to his position. Colin Powell answered:

> "I was blessed with a family that kept me in play. They wouldn't let me fall by the wayside even though I would have done it in a heartbeat if I did not have them. I sometimes use the metaphor of a pinball machine. You know, you shoot this ball out, and out comes this kid, and the kid goes bouncing around the pinball machine, and heading into the holes that take you nowhere, and just about the time you're about to slide off into nowhere, the flippers kick you back into play. That's your parents, your cousins, your peers, your teachers, your coaches, your ministers, and your rabbis. Kids need adults to keep them in play while they're figuring out where they want to go."

V. 6.

(Graham. 2006, p.82)

Today, in the second half of life, where it is possible to live past seventy years of age, we have been given the gift of years to address these earth-shattering questions. How does one establish a relationship of trust? What is there to hope for? Where does one find purpose and meaning in a world hell-bent on destruction? It is the individual who must lead the way. The adult individual must be taught "to listen to his/her own nature" so that s/he can understand from within what is happening.

Listening to one's own nature, taking into one's self that which is projected onto others is crucial to maintaining an individual's life energy into the later years. Through that individual life, "something" is left in this earthly world for the next generation.

> "A human being would certainly not grow to be seventy or eighty years old if his (or her) longevity had no meaning for the species."

(Jung. C.W. Vol. 8, p.399)

In this twenty-first century, the individual with an extended life span has the opportunity to make a contribution to a humane life for future generations.

THE WHEEL ~ EXPLORING YOUR CORE ENERGY
Activity Form

Purpose

To first look for what energizes you ~ the wheel that keeps you moving! And then, to use that knowledge to decide how to hold onto your individuality while connecting with those around you.

Materials needed
- Blank white paper
- Pen or pencil

Space needed

A place to write or a portable writing top (book, clipboard, etc.).

Number of people

Alone.

Options:

> Two or any multiple of two persons can engage in this activity.
> With an uneven number, have one group of three.
> (This activity can even be done at conferences with large rooms of people as long as the facilitator can be heard.)

Time necessary

STEP ONE	5 minutes
STEP TWO	5 minutes
STEP THREE	10 minutes
STEP FOUR	20 minutes
STEP FIVE	15-30 minutes

Desired outcomes

1. To look more deeply at your core themes/core values
2. To strategize ways to honor those themes
3. To strategize ways to eliminate draining patterns and/or ask for help
4. To offer a deeper discussion of what matters to individuals in a group
5. To energize a discussion of how to stay connected without eliminating individuality

THE WHEEL ~ EXPLORING YOUR CORE ENERGY
Experience

STEP ONE

Draw a circle in the middle of a piece of paper.

- The circle should cover less than half of the surface of the page.
- Inside the circle draw six lines that meet at the center and go out to the circumference of the circle.

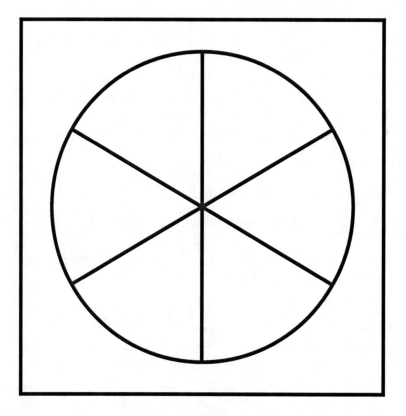

STEP TWO

Write each of the following words on one of the six internal lines:

- Food
- Clothing
- Activity
- Location
- Space
- People

STEP THREE

Complete the next few directions by answering fairly spontaneously. There might be many answers to each question. Just choose "one" ~ preferably the first one that comes to mind.

- At the end of each line, right outside of the circle, write the answer to these questions (correlating to the six internal words above):
  - What is one of your favorite foods?
  - What is one of your favorite pieces of clothing?
  - What is one of your favorite activities?
  - What is one of your favorite locations in the world?
  - What is one of your favorite safe spaces to be occupying?
  - Who is one of your favorite people?
- Write three words to describe each of your answers.

STEP FOUR

Review all of your answers in Step Three.

- Where do you see connections between your answers?
- Did you use any of the same words to describe each?
- When you look at these answers collectively, what jumps out as similar?

When working with others, allow one person to share his/her entire wheel without making comments, like "Oh, I wrote that too," or "How interesting!" Just sit and actively listen. Only after you have absorbed all of your partner's answers should you then reflect back what you have heard and what you see as important to him/her.

Whether working alone, with a partner, or in a small group, end Step Four by <u>choosing three words or phrases that articulate what is important to you</u> ~ **core** themes that run through these answers.

STEP FIVE

Explore how these **core** personal themes shed light on a current goal you are trying to achieve or a challenge you are facing.

- What do your three themes tell you about yourself?
- Do your themes help you see what absolutely must be done for a satisfactory result, versus what can be eliminated or at least set aside as secondary?
- Do you see how the themes are playing out in the steps you are taking?
- Is there a task you are facing that would be much more manageable if you asked for help? If so, what actions do not directly connect to your themes? Those actions outside of what is most energizing to you would be initial places to solicit help.
- Are you able *not* to do some step, realizing that it is an expectation, not a necessity?
- When you think of times in your life when you feel happy or successful, are these themes present? If so, where do you see them? In objects around you? In activities occurring?

QUESTIONS FOR REFLECTION

- What would it be like to use your core themes to set future goals?
- When you get into difficult situations, what expectations "hook" you and how can understanding these themes help you to eliminate steps or to ask for help sooner?
- How can you use this exercise to understand conflicts within yourself?
- How can this exercise help you to learn about others and/or to resolve conflicts with others?

BEING VICTIMIZED DOES NOT WARRANT BEING A VICTIM!
Ma & Me Story

When Ma and I worked together, I often watched the audiences' reactions.

First, they would wake up and really listen. She was a bit different from typical trainers. She didn't have a beautiful workbook for them to follow, step-by-step. What she did have was a long life ~ full of fabulous stories! And when she told those stories, the participants were on the edge of their seats. Here was a woman full of energy in the fourth stage of her life. She was an example of living life to its fullest and not becoming a victim of old age, cultural abhorrence of aging, or the internal fear that she had nothing else to offer. On the contrary, she was there because she was drawn to share what she had learned and to pass it on.

Most presentations would start as the beginning of this chapter did. She would share her three messages:

1) The Victim Question,
2) The Need for Trust and Hope, and
3) The Search for Purpose and Meaning.

Within a few minutes, she would be totally engaged, and that engagement would elicit a story from her life. In other words, a story would pop in her mind, and off we would go on a "tangent!"

One of the audience favorites was the story of "Peg."

Pauline grew up Sicilian in a predominantly Irish neighborhood. For most of her childhood she tried to fit in, liking the foods her friends ate and bringing as little attention to her "Sicilian-ness" as possible (kind of like me pretending that she and I were not related . . . good luck!)

She auditioned in high school for the play "Peg of My Heart." She loved to sing and dance, and really wanted the lead part. She didn't get the part. One of the teachers told her that although she was the best in the audition, she didn't look like Peg (i.e., she wasn't Irish!).

Well, she wasn't going to let them get the best of her. She took a role in the chorus and spent the entire play cutting up and getting all the other performers to laugh constantly ~ including those on stage! As she puts it, "I was terrible!"

On some level, this is just the "sour grapes" behavior of a teenager. But reflecting back in her seventies, Pauline talked about how difficult her youth was and how determined she was not to become defined and controlled by those difficulties. Her family was very poor, she had a sick younger brother who required special care (until his death at age thirteen), and her father was in and out of their lives battling his own illnesses. He died shortly after his son.

But Ma was determined not to give up.

In her senior year of high school, she attended night classes at the Pittsburgh Beauty Academy. She graduated from high school and "beauty school" at sixteen. One year later, at the age of seventeen, she purchased beauty shop equipment on a monthly payment plan, assumed the financial responsibilities of the household, and took her mother from church janitress to independent beautician.

After a year of studies, her mother received her beautician's license. When Ma married at nineteen years of age, her mother was an accomplished beauty operator, running a thriving business.

(As I am writing this story, Ma is trying to get me to take it out of this workbook. She loves telling these stories in person, but not necessarily seeing them in print, where they will live on! So, I will switch from her story to my experience of her teaching me not to be a victim of my situation.)

My childhood was very different than my mother's. I grew up in an affluent suburb, and by the time I came into the family it was financially very comfortable. I also got a great deal of encouragement at home and in the community to develop my talents. I played the guitar and sang, went to acting classes, and believed I could do just about anything I put my mind to.

In junior high school, I ran for student council. We had to go from class to class, talk about why the kids should vote for us, and then make a final speech in front of the whole school before they voted.

I wanted to use my talents and do something a little different. I wrote a campaign song about my name, "Napier, meaning Na – Peer, meaning No – Equal." If I must say so, it was catchy!

I went from class to class with my guitar, singing away. I was nervous, but it pushed me to identify who I was and proved to me that I had courage.

When it came to the student assembly, the administration told me that I was not permitted to sing. They said it wasn't fair. The other competitors didn't have this talent, and it wasn't how things were traditionally done.

I was really upset, and Pauline was livid! She rarely intervened in our school issues. She felt that we must learn to work through our own conflicts ~ but this was an exception!

She dressed up in her nicest outfit (always look good when you are confronting the dragon!). She went to the school and met with the top administrator.

She was gracious and polite (watch out, here comes "Peg!").

"I'm sure you understand, Mrs. Napier, that we can't show bias. If we let Michelle sing, we must let everyone sing," he explained.

"But everyone doesn't want to sing, Mr. Y. Nor can everyone else sing and compose a campaign song," replied the demure Pauline.

"Exactly, Mrs. Napier. It isn't fair if one child sings unless all of them do. And we must be fair. You understand, don't you, Mrs. Napier?"

"Ah, of course I understand, Mr. Y," she said, purposely mispronouncing his name. "I understand mediocrity very well."

And unbelievably, his response was, "Oh, I am so glad you do understand, Mrs. Napier."

I didn't get to sing my campaign speech.

I learned that even if I am mistreated or blocked from achieving an important goal, I do not have to respond as a victim.

There are times you can't change another person's perspective, but you do not have to lose your own in order to move forward. This event was not about the administrator. It was about me ~ learning to stand up for myself and to move forward with pride. (I still ran for the student council office but don't remember whether I won. I do remember this story.)

This event stimulated a growing trust in myself ~ an understanding that I could tap my talents and try something new without falling apart. I could survive a disappointment without feeling victimized by it. I again experienced trust of my mother, as my protector against the established power structure. She showed me how to stand up and speak my mind without "rolling around in the mud" and becoming like my adversary.

Pauline was much further along in her trust-building journey too.

Unlike her childish derailment of "Peg of My Heart," in this situation, she was "strategic" to make sure I wasn't derailed and she held herself in check with the administrator.

She never tried to get back at him after that. And I continued singing and playing my way into adulthood.

CHAPTER IV
TRUSTING AN INVISIBLE ENERGY

TRUSTING AN INVISIBLE ENERGY
The Transcendent Function

How does one activate the energy for a newly creative life? Heraclitus proposed that no life could exist without the union of opposites. In human form, new life begins with an egg and a sperm, a mother and a father. From that zygote, a new infant develops and enters the world. Following Heraclitus (c.500 B.C.E.), Jung has said:

> "It is my belief that the problem of opposites . . . should be made the basis for a critical psychology. A critique of this sort would be of the utmost value not only in the narrower field of psychology, but also in the wider field of the cultural sciences in general."

> (Jung. C.W. Vol.8, p.125)

These opposites appear exclusive of one another. But if one can hold the tension of both sides without excluding one or the other, a third possibility emerges that may create a drastic change in attitude and action. In other words, if one could bring forth from a personal conflict the opposite meaning of the conflict and hold both sides, in that union, a third yet unknown entity emerges from the unconscious bringing a source of new energy. This process Jung termed the transcendent function.

> "I have called this process in its totality the transcendent function, function being here understood . . . as a complex function made up of other functions, and "transcendent" not as denoting a metaphysical quality but merely the fact that this function facilitates a transition from one attitude to another."

> (Jung. C.W. Vol.6, p.480)

59

"There is nothing mysterious or metaphysical about the term 'transcendent function.' It means a psychological function comparable in its way to a mathematical function of the same name, which is a function of real and imaginary numbers. The psychological "transcendent function" arises from the union of conscious and unconscious content."

(Jung. C.W. Vol.8, p.69)

" . . . the (person) would like to know what it (the pain) is all for and how to gain relief. In the intensity of the emotional disturbance itself lies the value . . . In order, therefore, to gain possession of the energy that is in the wrong place, he must make the emotional state the basis or starting point of the procedure."

(Jung. C.W. Vol.8, p.82)

"The shuttling to and fro of arguments and affects represents the transcendent function of opposites. The confrontation of the two positions generates a tension charged with energy and creates a living third thing . . . a movement out of the suspension between opposites, a living birth that leads to a new level of being, a new situation."

(Jung. C.W. Vol.8, p.90)

And lastly, but quite importantly, Jung continues:

"It is a way of attaining liberation by one's own efforts and of finding the courage to be oneself."

(Jung. C.W. Vol.8, p.91)

Because of Jung's discoveries, my analysands and I searched for ways to implement the process he describes. While we found many examples of the transcendent function at work, we could not find a repeatable discipline for approaching the complexities that Jung presented.

A few years later, together with another analysand, a process for engaging the opposites became a starting point for activating the transcendent function. We named it *Transformation Process Over Time: A Five-Step Model* (see Chapter VI for further discussion).

The moving back and forth to opposite positions, conscious and unconscious, the I or the not-I, opens a channel of energy flow that is capable of creating a yet-unknown third. It is an "And-Both" synthesis. The exclusiveness of "Either-Or" nullifies creation. This "And-Both" approach, psychologically speaking, generally makes its appearance in a seemingly threatening form. Consciousness, that is the ego at the center of consciousness, has worked long and hard at maintaining self-esteem and self-preservation. These qualities are absolutely essential for receiving the unknown, the unconscious. If one has no tolerance for this threatening aspect, the prospect of bringing a change of attitude into one's life seems unattainable. If one cannot house the unknown energy, unconsciousness displaces consciousness; one's energy goes to the wrong place. At this point, consciousness and unconsciousness become disturbed. There are many instances of the transcendent function at work. Perhaps an example may clarify this concept.

During my years of practice, a chemical engineer (we will call him Daniel) came into my consulting room claiming a feeling of loss of energy, no longer interested in his position as head of a research project for a prestigious company, and a sense of morbidity. Daniel's technical expertise left little space for the acceptance of an "invisible energy," however he conceived it to be. He understood it to mean a belief in a religious entity and proceeded to put all of his energy into a particular figure. Daniel then followed an evangelical path, trying to enlighten everyone he came in contact with to his view of an "invisible energy" – including me. He simply switched his role as head of an intellectual research department to head of a moral evangelical ministry. For many months, we both worked very hard with communicating and understanding the dynamics that were being constellated. Both the conscious and the unconscious were being honored.

Then one day Daniel came into our session very excited. He said, "I know what you are talking about. You're talking about 'salt'!" During our many sessions, I could not remember any mention of salt or what meaning it could possibly have pertaining to the transcendent function. Then he said, "Salt comes from the combination of two destructive elements. When they are combined, they make salt."

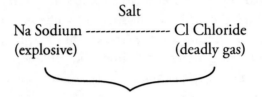

Salt
Na Sodium ----------------- Cl Chloride
(explosive)   (deadly gas)

Each by itself is lethal, but combined they produce NaCl or salt ‑ a new substance that enhances life.

The examples that registered for me in the understanding of the transcendent function (e.g., childbirth) had intellectual meaning for Daniel, but had little experiential meaning for him. Daniel's understanding of the transcendent function came from a scientific, chemical metaphor — his own knowledge and history. Meaning must come from one's own knowledge and history.

At times, going through this process brings with it dramatic, energetic changes in one's situation. It is a method of "embodying liberation by one's own efforts." During this process, an "invisible energy" comes out of one's unconscious into the individual's conscious realm. With the union of conscious and unconscious content, "a living birth, a new level of being, a new situation" enters the light.

Taking these experiences from the private consulting room into the outer world (business, health care, etc.) became the creative task of Michelle's work.

A Passport Introduction to the Opposites
Activity Form

Purpose
To create a visual snapshot of who you are at this point in time, including examples of opposites through which you filter the world.

Materials needed
- A journal for each person
- Blank white paper
- Crayons, colored pencils, or paint
- Scissors (optional)
- Glue or tape
- Music (optional)

Space needed
Flat surfaces (tables or the floor).
Depending on the number of people, a bit of room to spread out to draw.

Number of people
When done alone, find a trusted friend to complete Step Two.

Options:

> Two or any multiple of two persons can engage in this activity.
> With an uneven number, have one group of three.
> (This activity can even be done at conferences with large rooms of people as long as the facilitator can be heard).

Time necessary

STEP ONE	20 minutes
STEP TWO	30 minutes
STEP THREE	15 minutes
STEP FOUR	30 minutes
STEP FIVE	10-60 minutes

Desired outcomes

1. To take time to reflect on how our personality and the opposites within it impact our current walk
2. To acknowledge where we feel competent and joyful and where we feel incompetent and uncomfortable
3. To experience the world for a moment when our strengths "go too far"
4. To build understanding that opposites create wholeness and new creations!

A Passport Introduction to the Opposites
Experience

STEP ONE

Write down:

      A. Something you <u>love to do</u>.
      B. Something you <u>are very good at doing</u>.
      C. Something you <u>do not like to do</u>.
      D. Something you <u>are not very good at doing</u>.

Take a white sheet of paper and divide it into six sections, by folding the paper like a letter in an envelope and then in half.

A. love	C. do not like
B. very good at	D. not good at

On the left put your favorable examples in the first two boxes.

On the right put your unfavorable examples.

Now, draw a picture at the bottom of each column that symbolically reflects your answers in that column. For instance, if I said that I love to sing and I am good at organizing my time, I might draw musical notes in a nice line or a circle with stars in a beautiful pattern. The picture you draw does not need to be aesthetically beautiful or clearly understandable. It is important that when you look at the picture you see a bit of your answers ~ the energy, attitude, activity, or impact of those answers.

After completing the drawing in both the left and the right sides, fold the written answers under so that the pictures are on top and the writing is underneath/in back.

STEP TWO

Pair up with a partner/friend and allow him/her to look at your pictures only.
Ask what s/he sees in the picture, and what answers might be written in the top two boxes in each column, reflecting those pictures.
After s/he has a chance to respond, share your written answers.
Do this for both the left and the right of each person's sheet.

In this discussion time, talk a bit about your answers and reflect on how those answers manifest themselves in your personal life, professional life, community activities, etc. Where and when do you feel competent and joyful? How would you define the feelings on the "negative" side? What happens to your ability to trust yourself or others when you are engaging in activities on either side?

STEP THREE

After the discussion, take your own sheet and cut or tear off the two sections with the pictures. Then glue or tape each picture inside to the two blank, facing pages of a journal.

These two pages are the front inside cover of your current life's passport.
It represents a snapshot of you at this time.

Your strengths and your weaknesses, your loves and your dislikes, and what you see as positive and what you see as negative are briefly expressed in this snapshot.

You may name the current "passport" or the journey you are currently on.

This passport is now an introduction to:

- Looking at your talents and gifts
- Exploring your personality ~ where your greatest sense of compentence and joy resides as well as areas in which you are challenged and uncomfortable.

STEP FOUR

Here is an additional step that has helped me understand "holding the opposites."

I call it *The Square.*

- Draw a box. Take what you have written in "very good" at doing (Step One), and put it on the top left corner of the box. Now think about what that talent/gift looks like when it goes too far.

  For example: I always talk about having a great deal of energy in a workshop. When that energy "goes too far" it becomes frantic and hyper. (See diagram following Step Four)

  - I'm sure most of you have heard the expression: "Our greatest strengths can also become our greatest weaknesses." That is what you are trying to identify here ~ when does your talent/gift go from a strength to a weakness?

  - Now you have another "opposite" to hold and consider. Do you know when this occurs for you? What sorts of situations or issues push you to the far right side of the box?

- To continue with this analysis, identify a couple of actions you take to pull back from the extreme of that talent/gift. (Again, with my example, I literally tell myself to breathe deeply three times. I also create a question for the workshop participants to consider in small groups and force myself to listen carefully to their responses . . . I sort of give my energy talent a "time out" and ask the group to supply the energy.) Place in the lower right corner of the box what your talent looks like as you pull it back from its extreme.

- Then, consider what will happen if you continue with the "pull back" strategies. (If I continue asking the group questions and only listen, I abdicate my responsibility for giving the workshop direction. My energy gets pushed to the side and I no longer lead.) Describe what this situation looks like in the bottom left corner of the box. This description is probably the true opposite of your original talent/gift.

- Finally, consider what actions you can take at this point to pull your talent/gift back to the forefront. (When I feel myself losing my ability to energize the group, I set a clearer direction and concrete outcomes and then drive the group forward. I often use what they have told me in the discussion to identify what is most important at this point. I have to find a way to re-energize myself and take the reigns again. It is not about my talent "shining;" it is about my talent working to help the group.)

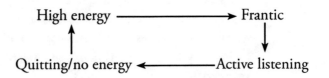

When we rely too heavily on our strengths, we have the potential to poison our good intentions. Anything taken to an extreme has the probability of becoming its opposite, *enantiodromia*. (Jung. C.W. Vol.8, p.219)

If we begin to develop consciously the strength to "hold the opposites" in ourselves, we can increase our ability to hold the opposites all around us and avoid functioning from an extreme position.

This increased capacity is crucial to trust-building. Instead of allowing a good thing to go to an extreme and turn into a negative force, we become better at managing our strengths and talents. Sometimes, we experience personal "salt" situations ~ holding the opposites and transcending to something new.

STEP FIVE

Take a moment to look at the passport snapshot before making new entries in your journal. Answer one or more of the questions posed in the accompanying *Activity Form*.

QUESTIONS FOR REFLECTION

Encourage yourself to find multiple and potentially "opposite" answers.

- Where are you are at this point in your life?
- Where do you want to go?
- What do you need to move forward?
- What are your reasons for going?
- How does this "passport" help you travel through this workbook (as a literal passport allows you to travel away from home)?

A Personal Numinous
Moment of Trust ~ Sicily
Ma & Me Story

We had dreamed of going to Sicily for years ~ walking and smelling the same earth that our great-great-grandmothers had known ~ tasting the bread and wine of the land. Pauline had pioneered there first. She went alone in 1982 when she was writing her thesis on Demeter and the Black Madonna. Her stories had permeated the air with energy and awe.

Finally, after a couple years of saving and planning, I went with Pauline and two of my sisters. We landed in Sicily on Good Friday, 2005. Among the many, many stories from that trip, this one left an unforgettable impact ~ a memory of self-trust and of an invisible energy permeating the space, a group of strangers, my sisters, Ma and me.

We awoke toward the end of our vacation to a beautiful day in Taormina, a city perched high above sea level. The sky alternated between clouds and sun and created shadows on the sea below. The four of us went to the hotel's rooftop restaurant for breakfast. We ate mouth-watering cheeses, breads, olives, and dried fruits while drinking coffee. We were relaxed and engaged ~ soaking up each other's company and taking in the sights, sounds, and smells.

After discussing the gifts each of us still needed to purchase, we decided to split up, shop, and meet again at midday in the Teatro Greco. I decided to challenge myself. I knew that the best shopping would be found off the beaten track. So I walked up the narrow side streets, away from the crowds.

I was a bit nervous. There was no sense of danger, just a discomfort with the unknown. I encouraged myself to trust my instincts. I knew this discomfort was a mistrust of myself, not a valid worry of anything around me.

I came upon a wonderful ceramic shop and met its beautiful female proprietor/artist. I spent a long time at that spot. If I could have carried more, I would have bought enough ceramic tiles to redo my entire house! As it was, I chose a few precious small pieces, photographed the woman, and left happily.

Then, working my way back to the main tourist path, I found a "colorful" jewelry store. The jewelry cases inside were packed and it was difficult to find merchandise. It resembled an overstuffed materials closet in a classroom without storage space. In fact, the owner was a retired schoolteacher whose attire and demeanor reflected the store's ambience. We talked and laughed as I looked at her wares.

Pauline heard me from the street and walked in. Thirty minutes and many purchases later, Ma and I left the little store laughing and feeling quite pleased with our gifts. Now, with our shopping almost done, we continued up the hill to the Teatro Greco, a stunningly preserved ruin estimated to have been built in the Third Century B.C.E.

The stone street and stone walls of the structure drew us into a world that had withstood so much and was still "living" in the present. We climbed up and up and up ~ finally coming out into stone bleachers, overlooking the stage below and the grand sea and sky beyond! Oh, Magnificence!

We sat in silence and absorbed this moment.

It began to get cloudy, but I barely noticed.

And then, all of a sudden, we felt raindrops. Seeking shelter, we scurried to the top of the stone bleachers and each ducked into a small alcove, perhaps previously reserved for guards or for statues of powerful beings. My sisters had not yet arrived. So we saved room for them in our alcoves and waited.

I periodically talked with Ma as the rain came down. As I did so, I noticed the extraordinary acoustics and commented to Ma that this structure was built to carry the human voice superbly!

Of course Pauline asked me to sing!

My mind raced! There was no way! I was in Sicily in a very public place.

However, there was no one around. The rain had chased everyone away. Oh, heck. What could be the harm? We were basically alone and a song would make Ma so happy. We were in Sicily and I do love to sing and it was a fabulous theatre space . . . so, I sang.

The song carried everywhere. It was like singing in a huge shower ~ I didn't have to strain my voice. The sound floated over the seats, down to the sea below and the sky above.

I finished and peaked out of my alcove, giggling to Ma.

Then, something totally unexpected occurred.

From many of the alcoves, all around the theatre, heads popped out! We weren't the only ones escaping the rain. And these others began applauding my singing, requesting me to go on!

Oh, my.

Pauline was encouraging me too!

Feeling just a "little" embarrassed, I stepped out of my alcove, took a breath, and sang another . . . and then another, and another ~ a well-known gospel song, one of my favorite folk tunes, and more.

My sisters appeared below. The rain stopped and people started emerging into the open, not only from the upper alcoves but also from the tunnels underneath and to the sides of the stone stairs. I felt overwhelmed and decided to stop. My sisters stepped up, smiling and applauding.

I was starting to wind down from my performance when a young Italian woman approached me and insisted that I sing on the stage below.

My first thought was, "Absolutely not."

I was already feeling quite self-conscious.

I couldn't understand her individual words, but her message was clear ~ the acoustics were even better on the stage and I must go down there and sing.

After several exchanges, I finally agreed. I asked her what she wanted me to sing. She said the "Ave Maria."

It felt wrong to say no. As I made my way down toward the inner tunnels leading to the main stage, my entire body was shaking *and* energized. The physical sensation was so huge that tears were streaming down my face.

I made my way to the stage, as more and more people were arriving into the theatre, emerging from multiple tunnels and entrances.

There was no turning back. I walked out on the stage. The theatre was enormous from down there. I closed my eyes, and began singing the "Ave Maria." The key was a little low, but I managed through the song. And then, one more burst of energy . . . I raised the key and sang (belted) this glorious song one more time, with my eyes still closed, my arms raised up and out, and my heart reaching out to Ma, my sisters, the young Italian woman, the "audience," and the ancient spirits all around!

I finished. Applause rang out. I opened my eyes to see many, many people all around.

I slinked off the stage, totally wiped out. There in the wings was a young family – husband, wife, and twin toddler boys. They had been videotaping the event. My family came down and we all talked. Then a lovely couple from England joined us. You would have thought this little group of people might be friends for life. (I actually received a Christmas card from the English couple the next December.) The young Italian "cheerleader" and others walked by and thanked me.

After our conversations drew to a close, my sisters, Ma and I walked out of the theatre and next door into the luxurious Hotel Timéo for a glass of wine.

This event was a numinous moment – infused with grace. It was an experience of trusting myself to share my vocal gift and of trusting an invisible energy – propelling this event, carrying me along, and pulling me down to the stage as I shook and cried. This moment in time was both all about me *and* had nothing to do with me. I was as much an individual performer as I was a vessel for the energy inside that theatre.

With the trust of that community of strangers, my sisters, and Ma, an extraordinary moment of connection was allowed to occur. They were receiving my gift of song and I was receiving their gifts of support, recognition, and love.

Today, when I close my eyes and imagine standing on those ancient stones, I feel the trust. I feel hopeful. I know that experiences like this are possible ~ experiences that confirm a trusting connection to ourselves, to the invisible energy, and to those who walk alongside us.

CHAPTER V
TRUSTING OTHERS

PART ONE:
BUILDING TOLERANCE

TRUSTING OTHERS PART ONE:
BUILDING TOLERANCE
Transforming Conflict

The American Heritage Dictionary's (Fourth Edition) first definition of conflict is: "a prolonged battle; a struggle; clash." The third entry in the dictionary under conflict reads: "Psychology. The opposition or simultaneous functioning of mutually exclusive impulses, desires, or tendencies." The word "conflict" comes from the Latin confligere: com, together, and fligere, to strike. You can see from this minimal information that conflict is a complex human experience, one that calls upon a relationship to "oneself" and to the "other." In conflict, the relationship of oneself and the other is characterized by a struggle with mutually exclusive elements. Added to this conflict is the fact that these mutually exclusive elements (be they Na-Cl or male-female) alone cannot create a new "other." It is in conjointly having a relationship with one another that a newness unfolds. What a conundrum? Yes, it is a deep riddle of relationship, at the core of which lies trust.

When conflict arises, how does one address this riddle of relationship, particularly if trust was missing in the first year of life and, as Erikson points out, mistrust takes its place? Through Jung's work on what he termed the transcendent function, my analysands and I searched for methods to implement the process he described. The methods that were known usually involved the expertise of a professional analyst schooled in symbolism and a commitment of time and money from the analysand. We were searching for a method that would free the analysand from dependence on the professional, and with a reasonable expenditure of time and money, the analysand would learn how to process conflict on his/her own. Well, this struggle went on for many years. (See Chapter IV)

Then one day a person from Europe with a limited understanding of English, and I, with no understanding of the foreign language, sat together in my consulting room. English had to be the language through which we conversed. Grappling with this problem led to the following implementation of Jung's transcendent function. While transformation is the aim of the transcendent function, how does one engage the conflictive energy that arises from the opposites of one's consciousness and that which is unconscious, particularly when there is a mutually exclusive understanding of language?

Through both of our struggles with the language barrier, a level of trust opened between us. The frustration that blocked addressing the conflict that brought the analysand into the consulting room culminated in the development of a simple five-step model reflecting Jung's concept of transformation of attitude and growth from conflict. Jung's own words on the transcendent function supported this model.

> "Life has always to be tackled anew . . . it requires the solution of an individual conflict if the whole of his (her) personality is to remain viable."

> (Jung. C.W. Vol.8, p.72)

> "In order, therefore, to gain possession of the energy that is in the wrong place, he must make the emotional state the basis or starting point of the procedure."

> (Jung. C.W. Vol. 8, p.82)

TRANSFORMATION PROCESS OVER TIME: A FIVE-STEP MODEL

(Origin, see Chapter IV)

Emotion is your guide for the five-step process.

1. ACKNOWLEDGE

Recognize your emotions in a secret, safe way.

For this process, do not discuss your conflict with others. Acknowledge your emotions to yourself, regardless of how distasteful this may feel.

2. HOLD

Experience the emotion within your body, within your personality, within your singular life history. Complexes will surface, i.e., the necessary something to help make you complete. Continue to keep your own counsel in secret. (Complexes are emotionally charged ideas that become manifest in behavior. A complex may have destructive or morbid tendencies; it may also be the source of creativity.)

3. QUESTION

What is happening?

Does the conflict that gave rise to the emotion have validity? Does the emotional accusation have an element of truth? Why did the conflict arouse emotion - embodiment? Where within my life-experience does this emotion touch? Ask the How, What, Where, When, and Why.

4. TRANSFORMATION

Listen.

Listen to what has been revealed to you that you were unaware of before this search. Transformation engages the ego,

81

the body, and the soul. Transformation does not eliminate, get rid of, or ignore the conflict, but demands working through it.

"It is a way of attaining liberation by one's own efforts and of finding the courage to be oneself."

(Jung. C.W. Vol.8, p.91)

5. RESPONSE

Now is the time for you to act.

How are you going to respond to the situation? Your behavior, your actions, your response is more likely not to be destructive to your ego-body-soul or to the "other" involved in the conflict because a connection has been made to a trustful, embodied Self.

A Five-Step Process on the Labyrinth
Activity Form

Purpose

To process a conflict in a way that provides a chance for transformation without harm, and with the possibility of creating something new ("salt").

Materials needed
- Plain paper (3-4 sheets)
- Pen (optional colored pencils as well)
- Labyrinth picture (following Activity Form)
- Envelope

Space needed

A comfortable, safe place to write and reflect.

Number of people

Alone.

Time necessary

Preparation	15 minutes
STEP ONE	5 minutes
STEP TWO	5 minutes
STEP THREE	15 minutes
STEP FOUR	Variable (until you have listened enough)
STEP FIVE	5-10 minutes
Suggested Response	Variable

Desired outcomes
1. To process a conflicting situation privately and safely
2. To experience Pauline's Five-Step Process "in your muscles"

3. To introduce the labyrinth as a personal tool for reflection and transformation
4. To demonstrate what a "container for holding the opposites" feels like

Brief introduction to the labyrinth

This experience takes the framework of the labyrinth and helps you to process your conflict safely and privately within that container.
This ancient tool:

- is a unicursal path – there is only one way in and you retrace that path on the way out.
- has existed throughout time and throughout the world with many variations.
- contains sacred geometry and is incorporated into many cultures/spritual practices as a sacred walk, reflecting one's search for the invisible energy.
- symbolizes the inner and outer life journey, finding one's Center and then reaching out to give back the gifts and wisdom within that Center.

Labyrinths exist in hospitals, prisons, churches, retreat centers, etc. There are many books and websites that explain the labyrinth (see Bibliography).

Labyrinth ~ Chartres Cathedral Pattern

A Five-Step Process on the Labyrinth
Experience

PREPARATION

List some of the current challenges/conflicts that confront you at this time. Pick one that you wish to improve. This challenge can concern a situation and/or a specific person.

Take the piece of blank paper and pen, and write continuously about that situation/person for 7-10 minutes or until your hand gets tired. Allow yourself to let go. Don't direct your thinking. You may find yourself writing "nonsense" or switching to unrelated topics. The writing itself does not need to be done well. The pen should not leave the paper. Your objective here is to begin with this topic and then, allowing your thoughts to flow freely, simply transcribe that stream-of-consciousness.

STEP ONE

Stop writing and close your eyes.
Visualize the conflict.

ACKNOWLEDGE	Recognize your emotions in a secret, safe way.
	For this process, do not discuss your conflict with others. Acknowledge your emotions to yourself, regardless of how distasteful this may feel.

STEP TWO

Allow yourself to feel the emotions connected to this conflict. You may actually notice places in your body where the emotions express themselves ~ stomach, head, back, etc.

HOLD   Experience the emotion within your
                            body, within your personality, within
                            your singular life history. Complexes will
                            surface, i.e., the necessary something to
                            help make you complete. Continue to
                            keep your own counsel in secret.

STEP THREE

Go to the labyrinth picture (or a copy of it). Using a pen or colored
pencil, begin slowly tracing the path into the labyrinth, starting at the
open entrance at the bottom.

Initially, allow yourself simply to feel the emotions and thoughts arising
from steps one and two. You may pause at any time ~ taking deep
breaths to help support you.

Then, begin asking questions about the conflict.

QUESTION   What is happening?
                            Does the conflict that gave rise to
                            the emotion have validity? Does the
                            emotional accusation have an element
                            of truth? Why did the conflict arouse
                            emotion ~ embodiment? Where within
                            my life-experience does this emotion
                            touch? Ask the How, What, Where,
                            When, and Why.

It is important to note that asking yourself "opposite questions" is
essential. To find the questions, realize that you can shift any question
and ask it from multiple perspectives. For example, "Why does she
always embarrass me in meetings?" may become "Why am I embarrassed
by what she says?" or "Does she realize she is embarrassing me?" or
"Why do I respond (verbally or non-verbally) to her comments?" or
"What is she saying that 'hooks me'?" or "Do I ever try to embarrass
her?"

The questioning process is like a pendulum. You are swinging back
and forth, looking at the conflict from many sides and holding the
various answers within your body and within the labyrinth.

NOTE: You are not trying to solve the conflict at this time. You are not looking for the right answer at this time. You are expanding your view of the conflict and pushing yourself to experience it from multiple sides.

STEP FOUR

When you reach the center of the labyrinth, stop.
Stop asking questions; stop processing, and breathe.

TRANSFORMATION

Listen.
Listen to what has been revealed to you that you were unaware of before this search. Transformation engages the ego, the body, and the soul. Transformation does not eliminate, get rid of, or ignore the conflict, but demands working through it.

"It is a way of attaining liberation by one's own efforts and of finding the courage to be oneself."

(Jung. C.W. Vol.8, p.91)

STEP FIVE

When you are ready, begin retracing your path, back out of the labyrinth. From what you experienced, what do you think your response should be? Take whatever you receive/hear with you. Let that message inform you ~ how will you respond to this conflict in the future?

RESPONSE

Now is the time for you to act.
How are you going to respond to the situation? Your behavior, your actions, and therefore your response are more likely not to be destructive to your ego-body-soul or to the "other" involved in the conflict because a connection has been made to a trustful embodied Self.

A SUGGESTED RESPONSE

Respond by writing a letter ~ one that you may or may not choose to send. Take a clean sheet of paper and write a letter to the person with whom you are in conflict or the person who "feeds" the situational conflict you are in. Write as much or as little as you like.

Put the letter into an envelope, addressed to *you*, and then hold onto that letter for a while. This letter may, at a future date, be something that you want to give to the person in a peace offering. But wait, hold, and continue to process whether this interaction is necessary and transforming. Even though it may be very difficult, not sharing the letter and absolutely not sharing it with anyone other than the person to whom it was written, has the greatest potential for transformation. You are expanding your capacity to hold conflict and not feed it. Ongoing conflicts get stronger when we continually go for help, look for others to "be on our side," and assume that if we can just change the other person, the source of the conflict will go away. This exercise asks you to look deeply at your own "wholeness" and what this conflict is teaching you about *you*.

> Remember: A response may be to not respond. It may be that you change your participation in the conflict. When you are making a conscious behavioral choice, you are responding.

ADDITIONAL REFLECTIONS

There are many labyrinth designs including the Chartres Cathedral Pattern (reproduced in this chapter). Finding which design appeals to you will enhance your immersion in this experience. You may wish to research this amazing tool further, learning to draw various patterns and finding the one that connects with your aesthetic and spiritual perspective.

The following questions may shed further light on the conflict you just processed. These questions require you to look more closely at your personal roots ~ what has always frustrated you *and* helped you grow. (A pearl starts as an irritation inside a shell!)

- What activity has given you problems since childhood?
- What inability have you tried to hide or laugh off?
- What task has given you the greatest frustration?

- Where do you feel vulnerable, slow to grasp, stupid?
- With your superior intelligence and expertise, what simple task do you pass onto others to cover up your ineptitude?

Hold these thoughts and feelings. Let them germinate until you don't feel threatened by the conscious self-knowledge.

Know what to hold (i.e., keep secret) and what to reveal to others.

CARETAKING IN THE LAST YEARS
Ma & Me Story

Grandma Spamp, Pauline's mom, was part of my life from birth until 1999. She came to our house every other Monday and helped with the laundry and various household chores. She spent hours over the ironing board! I can recall the smell of starch as she carefully pressed my father's shirts and hung them on the clothesline in the basement. I would come home from school and read stories to her as she worked. We would talk about school, family, and what was important in life.

As she approached the last few years of her life, it became increasingly difficult for her to walk, iron standing up, and go up and down the steps with laundry. One of the grandkids or great-grandkids would carry a basket of clothes upstairs for her to fold . . . and put her special "touch" on them! She would sit in a chair and iron (as she watched her afternoon soaps). She cooked even when the pots got too heavy to lift.

Her joy was to care for all of us and always to welcome everyone into her home with a bowl of pasta and homemade bread.

In the following story, Pauline shares a glimpse of her caretaking experience for Grandma Spamp:

> My mother, Sarah, was ninety-three years old when she died, and for thirteen years prior to her death, I took care of her in our home.
>
> She and I are part of an extended family of Sicilian women. Many of these women lived into their nineties. Some spent a portion of their final years in a nursing home and died in those institutions.

Medical science had extended the average life span into "old age." During the 1960s and 1970s, nursing homes flourished. It became wise and an acceptable practice for an elderly family member to receive health care in government-run or commercially run nursing homes.

One day, one of my relatives said to me, "You are only keeping your mother at home because you are too proud to put her in a nursing home."

I was furious. For thirteen years, I had been taking care of my mother and she (the relative) had no idea what this was like!

I was so angry that I decided I wasn't going to talk with this relative anymore. Furthermore, I was going to make certain that she was not invited to my mother's funeral. I became very primitive. I mean the Sicilian primitive, "I'll turn the whole family against her," primitive. She'll know how furious the family is by the time I'm finished with her!

Well, then I stopped for a moment and took this extreme emotional reaction to her simple comment into the five-step process.

1. Acknowledge the emotion:
   First, I acknowledged my emotions privately. I never told my children. They would have joined in my furor because they were worried about me staying healthy as I cared for my mother through many critical incidents. (This is true of most caregivers ~ the caregiver has to stay healthy or s/he can no longer continue as a caregiver. And so often, they wear themselves down and then they need to be cared for as well.)

   As I was acknowledging my emotions privately, I also knew I had to keep these comments from my mother, the patient. My mother would constantly say, "Honey, you are doin' too much. Call the nursing home; put me somewhere." When people would call her and say, "Sarah, I'm praying for you," she'd say, "Don't pray for me, pray for my daughter. She's the one who has to take care of me!"

2. Hold it in secret:
So, I acknowledged my fury and I held it, in secret. I never told anyone until a long time after my mother died. I actually told it for the first time in a workshop to a group of executives. Holding in secret is extremely difficult. Human nature needs to share the burden of pain with loving others ~ to find relief in human exchange. One needs to follow one's self as to when to reveal and when to hold in secret. Like childbirth, to bring new life into this world too early or holding it back too long endangers life's creation.

3. Question:
While I was holding the emotions, they became embodied. Rapid heartbeats and a queasy stomach sent their messages. At this point, while still holding, I knew that questioning had to begin. "Why had this comment affected me so deeply? Why am I caring for my mother at home, through these critical medical situations?"

Of course this questioning hit my complexes . . . feeling inferior; feeling anything I did wasn't good enough; feeling I was a child immigrant who just didn't know how to do anything right, etc.

"Was that why this was bothering me? No," I told myself. "I'm beyond those feelings."

Oh, no! You never get rid of your complexes. These feelings pointed directly to why my relative's comments were bothering me to the point of experiencing physical symptoms. Amazingly, if you can tolerate the internal struggle, your complexes really are a lifelong source of energy!

So, I finally concluded that yes, the relative was right. I was proud. I didn't want my mother in a nursing home. And, yes, I was proud to know that I kept my mother at home, even though I knew down deep that if I became ill, my mother would of necessity go to a nursing home against my wishes. If I was going to fulfill what I needed to fulfill, and care for my mother at home, I had to be healthy too. I needed to go beyond "holding the emotions and asking questions."

4. Transformation:
   At this point of consciously acknowledging the part I played in the conflict, an unexpected transformation occurred. My ego consciousness, my body, and the core of my being were interacting with one another ~ creating me in a new way. It guided my actions ~ my response to the conflict.

Remember: "It (transformation of energy) is a way of attaining liberation by one's own efforts and of finding the courage to be oneself." (Jung. C.W. Vol.8, p.91 ~ see also Chapter V, Part One *Experience*)

5. Response:
   I did not respond by going to that relative directly. I did not respond by telling my husband or children. I did not respond by telling my brother or cousins. I did not respond by reaching out to those who would give me sympathy . . . even though it may have been comforting at the time.

I responded by *not* alienating this relative from the family. I invited her to my mother's funeral.

The irony is, I felt healthier. I felt better. I felt calmer. And I was relieved that my anger did not put my mother, the patient, through the agony of this conflict. The last thing she would have wanted was for our family to be disengaged from one another.

Even though I did not confront the relative directly, I did respond. I experienced a transformation. My actions allowed me to honor my mother, not just by caring for her, but also by caring for the cohesiveness of the family, which she worked her whole life to sustain.

The conflict, consciously processed within myself, was contained and transformed without creating a larger, long-lasting conflict within the family community.

Michelle's final thoughts:

Grandma Spamp's passing was extremely difficult and full of love. We took turns talking, reading, and singing to "Gram" in her last hours, as she moved in and out of consciousness in my parents' home. She died on Palm Sunday, March 28, 1999. The week between her death and Easter was both a public and a personal "holy week." Her funeral mass was attended by many friends and family ~ *all* participated in celebrating her compassionate life.

CHAPTER V
TRUSTING OTHERS

PART TWO:
CREATION OR DESTRUCTION

TRUSTING OTHERS PART TWO:
CREATION OR DESTRUCTION
The Individual's Effect on the Collective

With the foundational search for trust of oneself and trust in an invisible energy in process, one may reach out to trusting others, whether they be family, friends, community or a different culture. You can see why this task is taken up in the second half of life. To build a house before the foundation is laid results in destructive hopelessness. An attempt must be made to honor wisdom people – those who have lived through and can sustain the tension that bringing the opposites to consciousness can evoke. Perhaps the hopelessness and lack of trust that contaminates the world will find a source of healing in one's individual efforts to heal oneself so that each person can leave this earthly world with dignity and the sense that the time spent here on Earth had meaning. May we replace the high-rises for the elderly and eliminate the holding rooms for death.

There are many examples of individuals who have achieved the wisdom state. It is possible! To study oneself is a formidable journey. It is the foundation of the possibility of connecting with the entire universe.

"No matter what he does, every person on Earth plays a central role in the history of the world. And normally he doesn't know it."

(Coelho. 1993, p.167)

Of the multitudinous world-wide people who have achieved the state of connecting their individual stories of gaining trust of themselves and their personal invisible energy to a trust of others, three people have occupied my thoughts as I write this chapter: Carl Jung,

Eleanor Roosevelt, and Nicanor Perlas. Each of these individuals had a relationship with their childhood and family, their fellow workers, the culture in which they lived, and other cultures throughout the world.

Carl Jung (1875-1961), whose theories of the development of personality formed the foundation of this work, eloquently recorded his own inner search in his autobiography, <u>Memories, Dreams, Reflections</u>. For if a person cannot experience that of which he writes, his or her concepts of life become empty. If these empty concepts pass onto "others," they produce a disenchantment, a pall upon the Earth, a malignant deficiency of which the cure has not yet been embodied.

May each of us find the strength to pursue this inner search.

During my studies, different theorists presented their knowledge for serious consideration. In part I was in agreement with each of them. I wanted to believe them (e.g., Carl Rodgers). But there was something lacking for me and I did not know what it was. At the closing of my master's program, I read Jung's autobiography. I remember feeling a sense of "Now, this fits me!"

When a concept touches a world population and continues to live over time, it somehow houses itself in the individual and touches the core of humanity. Jung spoke of this phenomenon as an archetypal image ~ not the archetype itself, of which no man can claim knowledge, but of an image of that unknowable archetype that reveals itself to the individual.

Perhaps Jung's autobiography, written when he was in his eighties, will resonate with you ~ perhaps not.

Eleanor Roosevelt's (1884-1962) autobiography, <u>On My Own</u>, portrays her life after her husband, Franklin Delano Roosevelt, died (12 April 1945). Her role as First Lady of the United States came to an end. In her sixties, Eleanor Roosevelt spread her trust in the diversity of peoples in the United States to trust of others in foreign lands. Her life took on a quest of valuing all peoples in all cultures. She became known as the First Lady of the World.

President Truman asked Eleanor Roosevelt to serve as a member of the United States delegation to the first meeting of the United Nations General Assembly, held in London, January 1946. For seven years, she served as a member of the newly established Commission on Human Rights. She was instrumental in the founding of the United Nations International Children's Emergency Fund (UNICEF), committed to the welfare of children worldwide.

She made numerous efforts to establish trust among peoples and nations, playing a vital role as chairman in the United Nations' passage of the Universal Declaration of Human Rights, 10 December 1948. Several years ago I phoned the United Nations' bookstore, requesting a copy of the Universal Declaration of Human Rights. The Secretary-General of the United Nations' name and signature appear on the introduction page. Eleanor Roosevelt as chairman and the members of the commission do not appear in this small, 3.5-by-5-inch booklet, which houses the thirty articles of human rights. I can hear Eleanor Roosevelt's voice regarding this matter, "That is of no consequence. The Universal Declaration of Human Rights was accepted by the United Nations and that is what is important."

Human rights ~ that which is fundamental to all humankind ~ must be honored in order to maintain humane interaction among persons and nations.

Eleanor Roosevelt was orphaned at a very young age. She was shy and considered unattractive. It took many years for her to embrace trust. Late in the second half of her life, Eleanor Roosevelt played a central role in the history of the world.

Nicanor Perlas was born into the sheltered and privileged world of the few in the heart of the poverty-stricken Philippines. Around the age of eighteen he chose agriculture as a career to help the poor and oppressed of his country. His choice horrified his friends. They said that he was giving up a life of fame and fortune. Thirty-five years later, on 8 December 2003, in Stockholm, Sweden, Nicanor Perlas stood in the Swedish Parliament delivering an acceptance speech of gratitude for being honored as one of the recipients of the prestigious Right Livelihood Award for 2003. The Right Livelihood Award is conferred upon those individuals who struggle to create a better world for humanity.

Nicanor Perlas has received many awards, faced numerous conflicts, and survived death threats. He spoke of a feeling of deep inner trust and of the path upon which his life journeyed. His latest book in progress, <u>Spirit of Empire: Societal Revolutions of the 21st Century</u>, reflects his connection with an invisible energy. He has become known as the "farmer from the Philippines."

In his respect and trust of others, Nicanor Perlas became a member of the United Nations Environment Program (UNEP). Various programs of the United Nations sent surveys to many countries throughout the world. They asked, "What is wrong in the world?" The response was overwhelming. The Human Development Reports (HDRs) documented thousands of problems. These responses were sorted into four categories: Culture, Politics, Economics and Environment. From all of the responses in each category, the committee asked themselves, "What one word summed up the world's problems in each area? How does the world view these problems?"

The word was:

Culture - - - - - - - - - - ROOTLESS

Politics - - - - - - - - - - - VOICELESS

Economics - - - - - - - - - JOBLESS and RUTHLESS

Environment - - - - - - - FUTURELESS

The committee then strived to find one word that described <u>the</u> problem of the world.

The word is <u>MEANINGLESS</u>.

(Perlas. 2000) (Meade. 2004)

"MAN CANNOT STAND A MEANINGLESS LIFE"

(Jung. Face to Face, 1959)

If one experiences life as truly meaningless, one cannot trust oneself, trust an invisible energy, or trust others.

Words from Nicanor Perlas's 2003 Right Livelihood Award acceptance speech bear repeating:

> "I am introducing the discourse of 'spirit' back into social activism because the problems we face, dear friends, cannot be solved by the same kind of mind and heart that created these problems in the first place. We are in fact faced with very deep spiritual social problems, which require spiritual responses from us. Ordinary, secular, materialistic answers will not do. The plea for human rights, for example, makes no sense if we truly believe that humans are simply complex biochemical machines that we can alter, patent, and clone . . . the inner journey brought me here from the Philippines to Sweden tonight. (This work) taught me a valuable lesson that I have never forgotten, that in the impossible is the real; in the impossible is the future waiting to be born."

Nicanor Perlas, Eleanor Roosevelt, and Carl Jung courageously took their individual inner journeys into relationships with others around the world.

A Community Collage ~ Vision of Trust
Activity Form

Purpose
To create a visual representation of a trusting community.

Materials needed
- Large plain paper or poster board (flip-chart size is good)
- Magazines
- Scissors
- Glue or tape
- Instrumental music and playing device

Space needed
A flat surface on which to cut and paste.

Number of people
Alone or in a small group.

Time necessary

STEP ONE	15 minutes
STEP TWO	10 minutes
STEP THREE	10 minutes
STEP FOUR	20-30 minutes
STEP FIVE	5 minutes

Desired outcomes
1. To create a visual product of hope
2. To discuss actions that can bring us closer to that vision of trust
3. To explore what work the group can do collectively and what is still an individual's responsibility
4. To provide an experience of a trusting conversation within oneself or within a group

A Community Collage ~ Vision of Trust
Experience

STEP ONE

Holding onto the images that have surfaced in earlier experiences (the childhood maps, the stories of trust, the labyrinth walk), begin looking through magazines for images that reflect what you have thought, felt, known, and experienced as trustful.
Do this in silence or with instrumental music in the background.

STEP TWO

Cut out these images, and begin arranging them on a large sheet of paper.

- If you are doing this with others, do not talk about your images or negotiate where to place them on the collage. Simply listen by looking and "feel" where your pictures fit amongst theirs.
- If working alone, sense the same "dance" within your internal dialogue. Try not to think about what is right; rather, allow the pictures to find their connections.

STEP THREE

Secure the collage with glue or tape.
View the collage and give it a title.

STEP FOUR

Now, sit back and process what you see:

1. With others, discuss this collage. What do the images represent in your vision of a trusting community? Listen intently to the explanations, looking for:

- Places where you have a strong similar perspective
- Places were there are distinct differences, in approach or outcome

Hold both similarities and differences. **Do not try to make what is different seem similar; that is part of each individual's capacity building ~ trusting even when there is not "sameness."**

2. If processing alone, write about these similarities and differences within yourself. Use the stream of consciousness writing ~ allowing your thoughts to jump and take you to unexpected places. Look for deeper understanding of the "co-existence of the opposites" within you. See if the collage can inform you on how this "vision of a trusting community" can also hold differences.

REFLECTION

As you create this picture and as you discuss it, understanding of commonalities and differences is to be welcomed. This is not an attempt to make the community in total agreement and homogeneity. It is an experience of what "staying separate and connected" might look like ~ how the similar and different pieces might co-exist.

If working in a group that functions at work, at home, and/or in the community together, this collage can serve as a vision of how this collective wants to experience its world. The next step for realizing some of this trusting community is to discuss actions that work toward this picture and actions that threaten it. The group may want to set a few norms or behavioral expectations ~ what do they need from each other in order to nurture this picture in their everyday working lives? If ideas such as "respect each other" arise, push yourselves to discuss what that looks like in *action*. How does each of you, through your individual personalities and life stories, show respect? What does each of you need to feel respect? These are not simple questions and they do not have one right answer. They are asking all community members to acknowledge their individuality/separateness and their communal connectedness.

NOTE: Each individual must also keep private some of what s/he thinks and feels (i.e., hold in secret). It is not the responsibility of the collective to care for the entire individual. The individual must first accept and care for himself or herself, holding his/her own strengths and weaknesses, beautiful parts and ugly parts, those unwelcome reflections that enter our consciousness as we open the door to listen. Until individuals do their own work and accept what they see in themselves, they cannot expect the group to take on that burden. If we abdicate our personal soul work, we begin to lose personal responsibility and personal power. Ultimately, that weakens the community and its potential for trust-building.

STEP FIVE

Find a special place to hang your collage. Allow it to "work its magic" in that space, reminding you of a hopeful vision of trust and bringing you imagery to energize your trust-building work.

SO ~ FOLLOWING THE RULES
Ma & Me Story

So, here we were, smack-dab in the middle of a three-day business retreat. Pauline and I were working with a third facilitator, Rob, and our clients, owners of a family business. The workshop had been exciting and intense.

Those who have worked in family-owned businesses have more than likely experienced both unbelievable challenges and rewards. These professionals live with less distinct boundaries between home and work. They interact throughout the day with the people who have known them from adorable innocence, through "lovely" teenage years, and into adulthood. Long-term interpersonal patterns have been established and often exist unconsciously.

Wait a minute . . . I'm talking about Pauline and me, too!

So, back to the three-day offsite . . . this was a multi-layered event ~ a mother-daughter team, working with a family unit, plus a non-related (but much trusted) co-facilitator. Everyone in the room was aware and functioning from this multi-layered perspective. Each person seemed to be drawn to one of the facilitators, and all three of us were talking throughout the workshop segments as well as at breakfast, lunch, dinner, and through each break. (By the way, this is not uncommon in our line of work. I usually have to force myself to take a "bio-break" or else I'm in the middle of a very intense group discussion and all of a sudden feel extremely uncomfortable . . . you get the picture!)

So, we were more than halfway through the three days and we designed an exercise to help the participants see what steps they were most committed to in order to move their business forward. All three facilitators agreed to a *very clear process* for the exercise. The exercise resembled one that you may have participated in at company workshops ~ each participant was being forced to "vote" on specific issues and, for the sake of the exercise, could not vote "maybe" or "only if." Only a yes or no vote would do.

The workshop participants were divided into three groups. Each facilitator was to work through the exercise with one of the smaller groups, following our established rules.

So, my small group was making excellent progress. Right in the middle of our allotted time, I got an idea about how to revise the process in order to get an even better outcome. (Remember, this is my strength ~ developing exercises in the moment to help people experience the change they desire and to create cooperative agreements.) My group was very pleased. We couldn't wait to come back to the large group and share our revised process and fabulous results!

So . . . wait! An obstacle emerged!

When my small group returned to the large group, I explained how we had improved upon the process. Pauline stopped me, exclaiming, "You can't do that, Michelle! We all agreed that we would follow these steps. You didn't follow the same rules that you insisted upon at the outset."

"But, Ma, we just discovered this shift in the rules, and it works so much better and will help all of us go a lot further right now!"

"Well, if I knew we were allowed to change things, I could have done the same thing. But I stayed within the rules and your group has to, too," stated Pauline with the authority of a mother.

"I didn't plan on changing the rules. This happened because the group began to have such a wonderful sense of synergy, and it was fabulous," I argued with the annoyance of a child who likes the way she rearranged the family's living room without the permission of her parents!

"I'm sorry, honey, but this changes the results of all the groups' answers. I'm sure everyone in the other two groups would have liked to have had the flexibility that you gave your group. Plus, expecting each of us to follow the rules that *you* designed, and then going off and changing them, is not okay."

So, in my head, I was thinking, "This isn't good . . . dah!"

I knew that the work my small group did was very productive and our results would positively impact the whole organization. I also knew that Ma was ticked. Like me, she hated following exact rules. But she did so to be a good team player and it wasn't easy for her. In addition, we were trying to get the entire group to make agreements and then stick to them, to trust that they would follow their agreements whether they were together or not. My taking liberty with the exercise, at a time when the entire group and both of us were exhausted, pushed the room into an uncomfortable moment.

We knew we were tired *and* we knew we were both "right."

We had had many such "fights" designing workshops together. Actually, we had had many such "fights" throughout our lives. This was really not a big deal to us. Sure, it was uncomfortable and neither of us wanted to back down, but it would not destroy our trust of each other or our working relationship. Many, many times before this, Pauline had complimented me for my ability to think on my feet and revise an agenda/exercise/discussion questions to respond to the energy in the moment. This is connected to my improvisational theatre training. Likewise, I had admired from day one the integrity that fills every cell of her body. When she agrees to something, you know she will not betray you. She is extremely loyal to her word.

As we looked around at the group at this offsite, everyone was nervously watching us. The eldest member of the family chastised me for disrespecting my mother! As the conflict expanded from a mother-daughter spat to a tension-filled room, we took a breath and proceeded. Pauline and I discussed openly with them what had just happened and how this might periodically happen within their family business. We also assured them that our relationship wasn't harmed by this disagreement. We didn't have to duke it out until one of us "won," but we did have to acknowledge that it was not helping the workshop move forward and that we had to compromise.

You may be wondering how we reached a compromise.

I relented. Rob had followed the rules too, and no matter how "brilliant" my revised process was, the group needed to know that when they agreed to something in their business, they needed to stick to it.

The wonderful blessing in this event, *totally* unorchestrated by Pauline or me, was the client's experience of watching us disagree. The group saw us realize the impact of our fussing, shift our attention, reflect on what just happened with those in the room, acknowledge how it happened, make a compromise, and laugh about it later.

And we very consciously did not get back at each other as the workshop continued. To keep a relaxed atmosphere, we joked about following the rules. **The combination of the number of times we had complimented each other's strengths plus the times we privately and courageously sat with each other and talked through our disagreements made us stronger here.**

This ability to negotiate a trusting relationship stems from a lifelong journey of walking your own path while staying connected to individuals around you. To this day, we have moments like this. Sometimes I am more exhausted and Ma leans my way. Sometimes I lean her way. Sometimes we are both too exhausted and we take a break, knowing we will come back together when we have the energy. We know that we do not want or expect support that causes the other woman to lose trust in herself. We know how critical it is to honor the gifts each of us brings to a situation. And, most importantly, we know there will be times when we must allow the other person to walk away for a bit. There is enough experienced trust between us. We know that we will do anything for each other *except* give up the trust in ourselves. We don't expect it and we don't ask for it. We are individually responsible for holding onto our own perspective while treasuring the connection between us.

SECTION THREE:
MOVING FORWARD

CHAPTER VI
THE POWER OF OUR PRESENCE

THE POWER OF OUR PRESENCE
What Happens When this Work Is Not Done?

One has no sure formula for connecting the past and the future in the present. But, if one brings the totality of who one is into the reality of the present moment, then whatever the future outcome of one's past actions (whether those past acts are condemned or honored) the individual does not die in the face of adversity. One may find the "courage to be oneself."

Self-knowledge with a connection to an invisible energy brought into community, whether it be family, neighborhood, or the workplace, supports the possibility of bringing a trustful you (regardless of professional or socioeconomic status) into the moment.

Several examples of connecting the past and the future in our present come to mind.

At my mother's wake, an old woman from a working-class family with very little money, frail, leaning on the arm of her son (who said that she insisted on coming even though she was not well) told me of a remembrance of Sarah. When the woman was a young girl, her father died. He died during the Great Depression of the 1930s. The woman said, "I can still see Sarah walking up the sidewalk," a treeless, grassless street, "her arms filled with her homemade bread for our grieving family."

Sarah's first attempt at bread-baking was a disaster. It was hard and tasteless. The reality of her situation at the time was that she could not afford bought bread. So she tried and tried again to bake bread with the quality of flour and lard that was allotted to indigents.

Sarah became a superb bread-baker. She baked bread for any fundraising organization that asked, regardless of their affiliation. She taught her grandchildren, great-grandchildren, nieces and nephews, schoolchildren, neighbors, and retired persons how to make her now-famous Sicilian bread. She was once nominated for the volunteer of the year award by the City of Pittsburgh. She wrote back and thanked the committee for the nomination, but she could not attend the award dinner because she was committed to bake for a local fundraiser.

Yesterday, 2 February 2007, I was at our local library returning an armful of books. A doorbell rang. The librarian excused herself and hurried to unlock a side door. An older woman entered, bundled up against the below-zero weather, brave enough to hazard the winter winds, with her cane to steady her. She followed the librarian inside. I thought that the woman must be a volunteer at the library. How delightful to see a committed elderly person, with supportive cane, venturing out in frigid weather. As she turned to the gate behind the librarian's counter, she said, "You are Sarah's daughter, aren't you?" At first, I did not realize that she was speaking to me. But quickly I turned to her and said, "Yes." She said, "I think of Sarah so often. She taught me to make bread. I mixed it in a tub," she laughed. "Sarah was a very special lady. I think of her often." Apologetically, I said, "I'm sorry, but I don't know your name." She told me. I still haven't the slightest idea who she is or how she recognized me.

My mother, Sarah, died eight years ago. As I write I think: A past experience carried into the future through memory, created a meaningful encounter in the present. This phenomenon happens quite frequently - whether we are conscious of it or not.

Sarah was known as Gee, the Bread-Lady, and the Earth-Mother.

That is who she was - is.

Another example comes from a conference I attended. One of the speakers was a woman who was involved in brain research at Harvard University. The speaker said that one day she was fine, and the next day, while preparing for work, she felt bodily symptoms with which she was very familiar because of her research. She was experiencing the first symptoms of a stroke and was able to dial for help before collapsing.

The days ahead were otherworldly. She recognized no one, including her mother. Her intellectual brain lost all connection. Her intuitive brain, however, became acutely alert. When anyone entered her hospital room ~ doctor, nurse, housekeeping personnel ~ she knew immediately the intention of the person, whether to trust or distrust their motivation "for her."

After a period of time, while still in this state, her mother took her home. Her mother followed her daughter's pattern, e.g., the daughter would sleep for hours and hours, and her mother would not wake her to bathe or feed her. When through signs (for she could not speak), the daughter would indicate that she was hungry, etc., her mother would then respond.

At the conference, that daughter was lecturing with fine intelligence and humor to a group of approximately two hundred persons on her research of the brain from both a personal and professional perspective. Her emphasis on healing was on the important relationship of the intuitive-emotional brain to the cognitive-rational one. Both are necessary. However, in crisis, emotion was the guide.

In the foundation of these stories, we can feel/see the relationship of the elderly woman with Sarah, the stroke victim with her mother. The humane relationship of the giver and the receiver was built upon trust. Trust that would carry them into the future.

If one does not or cannot do this trust-building work, the body and the psyche have free reign. Regardless of the number of years a person's body survives, giving up the work leads to tragedy. By that I mean that the person exists, but those many additional years of an extended life span in the 21st Century are personified by an unlived life.

During the ten years that I have been working with executives, I have met men and women ~ faced with incomprehensible new science and technology, weary of the corporate culture, no longer needed ~ who find themselves moving into a "nobody" position. Many in the second half of life are trapped in a life-threatening struggle. The community in which they live no longer honors them. Moreover, they have no strength to honor themselves. They become ill.

This illness is not the illness of the body deteriorating in old age. That is a normal, natural process. With scientific technology that keeps the body working ~ when seventy or seventy-five years of age is not considered to be old ~ where does illness come from? Why is health care extremely problematic? These are very complex questions.

Many concerned persons are addressing these questions. Much of their energy searches for governmental support, health insurance coverage, drug availability, and dietary and physical education. While all of these are important avenues of inquiry, what program is directed toward the development of the aging personality within the individual?

To this group of people in the second half of life, the question burns: "What happens when this work is not done?" I have witnessed individuals turn backward instead of forward. In my presence, their emotions have gone back to when they were "somebody," when they were needed, when they were honored. They live in the past. The present and the future have little or no meaning for them. Slowly, the psychological basis of Alzheimer's disease is planted in the brain. And the brain responds. This 21st-Century disease eliminates wisdom people.

The past and the future live in our individual, singular presence.

The importance of the individual is eloquently stated in the following quotes:

> "Look at all the incredible savagery going on in our so-called civilized world: It all comes from human beings and the spiritual condition they are in! Look at the devilish engines of destruction! They are invented by completely innocuous gentlemen, reasonable, respectable citizens who are everything we would wish. And when the whole thing blows up and an indescribable hell of destruction is let loose, nobody seems to be responsible. It simply happens, and yet it is all man-made."
>
> (Jung. C.W. Vol.11, p.48)

"The true history of the spirit is not preserved in learned volumes but in the living psychic organism of every individual."

(Jung. C.W. Vol.11, p.35)

" . . . the salvation of the world consists in the salvation of the individual soul."

(Jung. C.W. Vol.10, p.276)

"The great events of world history are at bottom, profoundly unimportant. In the last analysis, the essential thing is the life of the individual. This alone makes history, here alone do the great transformations first take place, and the whole future, the whole history of the world, ultimately spring as a gigantic summation from these hidden sources in individuals. In our most private and subjective lives we are not only the passive witnesses of our age, and its sufferers, but also its makers. We make our own epoch."

(Jung. C.W. Vol.10, p.149)

"Everything that happened, happened because someone, an individual, made a decision . . . the Holocaust is so big, the scale of it is so gigantic, so enormous, that it becomes easy to think of it as something mechanical. Anonymous. But everything that happened, happened because someone made a decision. To pull a trigger, to flip a switch, to close a cattle car door, to hide, to betray."

(Mendelsohn. 2006, pp.478-479)

Trust reaches beyond belief.
It becomes a reliance upon
one's own nature,
an invisible energy, and
the other ~ not of one's race, creed, or color.

Wishing you,
Beni Viaggiu!

ELDER ADVICE
Activity Form

Purpose

To elicit advice "through the muscles" from a beloved elder.

Materials needed

- Journal
- Optional
  - Clothing, shoes, jewelry of this elder and/or an object that respresents them to you
  - Materials necessary for engaging in one of the elder's everyday activities
  - Plain paper
  - Colored pencils or crayons
  - Play dough

Space needed

A place to draw and reflect & a place to do your chosen elder's activity.

Number of people

Alone.

Time necessary

STEP ONE	15 minutes
STEP TWO	20-30 minutes
STEP THREE	15-30 minutes
STEP FOUR	10 minutes
STEP FIVE	15 minutes

Desired outcomes

1. To experience "in your muscles" the world through an elder's activity
2. To listen to advice from someone who cared for you
3. To acknowledge the impact that the past has on the future in the present

ELDER ADVICE
Experience

STEP ONE

Write down the name of one or more elders to whom you were closely connected and in whom you saw great wisdom.

Choose just one, and note your answers to the following about that person:

1. What were a few of this elder's everyday activities?
2. Which of those activities did you observe?
3. During which activities did s/he exude joy? During which activities did s/he demonstrate competence?
4. How did s/he dress?

STEP TWO

After briefly answering these questions, allot a comfortable amount of time to engage in one activity from your answers above.

You do not want merely to participate in that activity; you want to step into his/her shoes for a bit of time and feel how it was for him/her to do that activity. Ways to help yourself:

- Put on clothing that s/he would wear – a typical garment; certain type of shoes; colors s/he loved; a piece of jewelry; etc.
- Allow yourself to imagine him/her in your mind – how s/he talked; how s/he moved; how s/he looked; etc.

Do the activity *as that elder*, seeing, hearing, and feeling his/her presence.

STEP THREE

Now record some response from this activity – how it made you feel; what memories it elicited in you; what reflections emerged regarding that elder's values; etc. You can record this response in a number of ways:

- Write in your journal for a bit of time (preferably in stream of consciousness mode, without judging or planning what you will write . . . simply allowing your thoughts to flow).
- Draw a picture of your response (drawing the elder, the activity, or a more abstract picture of how it felt to be him/her for a few minutes).
- Make a play-dough sculpture instead of a picture.

STEP FOUR

Close your eyes and settle into a comfortable position:

- Breathe deeply ~ in through your nose, focusing on the tip of your nose (five times).
- After each breath, repeat the name of your elder.
- Feel the presence of that person and ask him/her for advice:

"What can I do today to continue building trust in myself, in the invisible energy, and in others?"

Listen closely for his/her answer.

STEP FIVE

Bring that advice into your world.
When you open your eyes, you may wish to:

- Add the advice to your drawing;
- Write down the advice in your journal;
- Find an object or picture that can be placed in your space today to remind you of this advice.

Ask your elder to continue "advising" you and guiding you through this trust-building journey.

QUESTIONS FOR REFLECTION

This experience allows you to reconnect with and honor beloved elders.

- In addition to these daily activities, what other stories from their lives are in your memory ~ either as experiences you had with them or as stories that describe their legacy to you?
- Your life "stands" on their shoulders and their lives. Allow your trust-building efforts to root in the love and wisdom they gave you.
- If someone you have mentored was to do this exercise, what activity might s/he choose from your everyday activities and what advice would you share about trust-building with him/her?
- If your elder were to do this exercise, what activity might s/he choose from your everyday activities and what reflections would you share about trust-building with him/her?

Trust-building expands when the past and the future merge into actions in the moment!

To Whom Much Is Given, Much Is Expected!
Ma & Me Story

I'm sitting at my computer, two weeks before Christmas, overwhelmed with a list of tasks a mile long and a deep, strong desire to finish the first complete draft of this workbook! Pauline and I started this project in May of 2003. It is now December, 2006.

The question that fills my work is, "How much is enough?" How much do I need to do to do my part? How much do we add to this manuscript to make it valuable to readers, but not overwhelming? How conscious must I be to feel that I am "walking my talk" and not talking the walk that I want others to do?

I just got off the phone with Ma. We are both excited about the prospect of finishing this book and are hesitant to put it out there. We constantly struggle with the writing aspects. Is it clear enough? Are we succinct enough? Does the flow make sense?

And on a deeper level, is this work what we are being asked to do?

As always, we teach what we need to learn.

I am learning to trust myself. That requires me to believe that what I know as a professional facilitator is worth sharing and that it is only worth sharing if it comes from my experience. In other words, the concepts that we have put forth in this workbook and in our workshops are ideas, values, and expectations that both Pauline and I embrace ourselves.

Here's a good example. Just a few months ago, we were reviewing my story about Sicily, "A Personal Numinous Moment of

Trust." (Chapter IV) Ma really likes the story. But she pauses, and then gently comments that a few of the details in the story are incorrect.

I immediately feel defensive. I want to say, "This is my story. This is how I remember it. It isn't important to me if every fact is correct. What is important is the experience I had."

Knowing that Ma adored what I did and told everyone about it when we got home, I wonder, "Why am I getting annoyed with her extremely minimal feedback?"

Dah, I'm not good with details. I am receiving this as criticism because I am having trouble trusting my ability to recollect the event accurately. Ma's gentle question hits one of my "buttons." How can I be so sure of what I remember and be wrong? How can I write a book about trust-building and feel this conflict?

Fortunately, in this moment, I also trust Ma. We have built a relationship over half a century that demands our engagement in this uncomfortable conversation. That means I need to share with her not only my different view but also my difficulty in listening to her view of the event.

Someone else watching this conversation might say, "Oh, for goodness' sake, you two! Who cares if the Italian woman spoke English or not, and whether she asked for the 'Ave Maria' to be sung again? The point of the story is that she encouraged Michelle to go onto the stage and sing from there." (I can hear my siblings' exasperated voices in this comment, as they watch the intensity between Ma and me escalate. I can even hear my beloved maternal grandmother from heaven saying, "You both need a nap," or "Here, have a bowl of pasta!")

But Ma and I knew this feedback was not just about details. She did not want to irritate me, yet the detail changed the impact of the story for her. I did not want to bicker over a little point, but I wanted to tell my story *my way*!

We called one of my sisters on the phone to get her perspective. We were laughing, and we were fighting!

Okay . . .

So . . .

She supported Ma's version of the story.

And then something magical occurred! In this struggle something unexpected happened. I realized that I don't hear or see details when emotions are overpowering me. I literally can't remember whether that woman spoke English or whether she asked me to sing the 'Ave Maria.' I literally can't remember where my sisters were standing at that exact moment. I was experiencing something bigger than me, and by the grace of the invisible energy, I was fortunate to be with people I trusted and was literally in a safe, sacred space. The fact that my emotions took over in the Sicilian theatre was not only okay, but also necessary, for that event to unfold. Ma and my sisters were watching over me and I was not frozen by fear. I was able to offer a gift of love.

Pauline and I agreed that the story, "A Personal Numinous Moment of Trust," should remain written as I remembered it and this story would act as its complement. Together, the two stories show our individual perspectives and our process, rooted in trust, for finding acceptable common ground.

There is, of course, the other side of this magic. Just because I am not good at details does not give me permission to put the responsibility of the details on others. I need to work very hard at those things that do not come easily to me. This is how I build my capacity to hold the opposites within the world and within myself – this is how I build my strength to trust.

So, what is enough? Enough is in the moment. We take small steps that sometimes feel insignificant and sometimes feel extraordinary. The holding of our individual strengths and weaknesses and the continual work of looking deeper at that image of ourselves will, by the grace of the invisible energy, develop the wisdom we need to build trust in our world.

We are never done building trust. For each moment that we reach a new level of trust in ourselves, in others, or in the invisible energy, new challenges arise. Yet there is a "pearl of hope" that can begin to grow from these challenging irritations.

A courageous commitment to the practice of trust-building gives meaning to our lives and strengthens the next generation so that they can go a step beyond us! Hopefully, Ma and I have done enough here to offer something that will encourage you. The good news is that the work is difficult and rewarding, exhausting and exhilarating!

Below are the final paragraphs from the Ma & Me Tangent in Chapter I. It felt appropriate to reiterate the same message here.

Clearly, we are not advocating that all of you create a business relationship with one of your parents in order to implement the ideas in this book! We are advocating a conscious practice of building trust so that you may experience a personal and professional life that has energy and meaning.

Pauline and I have talked for long and seemingly endless hours about possibilities in the world - both the world we see and can touch, and the world of the imagination. I have had a number of excellent professional coaches. However, from that first time we presented a corporate workshop together, Ma has been my mentor and (as always) one of my biggest cheerleaders. She trusted that my gifts and ideas were powerful and that I needed encouragement for stepping up and sharing them with the world. I am grateful to the invisible energy for the gifts I was given at birth and for the motivating challenges that have appeared on this journey.

And I am profoundly grateful for Ma - for her heroic modeling behavior and her undeniable trust in me.

THE AUTHORS

Final Frame from "Human Strength: An Experience of
Trust & The Transcendent Function"
McKenzie Oaks Films

"Ma"

PAULINE SPAMPINATO NAPIER is a licensed psychologist in private practice in Pittsburgh, Pennsylvania. Pauline was born in Pittsburgh in 1928 and married in 1948. She has five children (Michelle is her fourth), twelve grandchildren, and one great-grandchild. Her husband, Tony, was the principal financial support for each family member's personal quest. All five of his children, as well as his wife, completed college and earned graduate degrees.

Pauline began her undergraduate work the year Michelle was born, 1957. While her primary efforts went to her family, she continued to pursue her education. It took her thirteen years to complete her undergraduate degree (1970). She then went on to earn her master's degree. It was in her last elective master's course that she was introduced to the work of Carl Gustav Jung (1972). During Pauline's Ph.D. work, her Jungian studies were continued through independent courses. At the final stage of her Ph.D. program (ABD [All But Dissertation]), Pauline felt compelled to travel to Zurich, Switzerland. After years of study in Switzerland, she completed the requirements of the C. G. Jung Institute, Zurich, for her "Diplomate in Analytical Psychology." She wrote her dissertation on "Demeter Of Villarosa, Sicilia – A Quality Of The Mother-Shadow."

Pauline Napier is a member of the International Association of Analytical Psychologists (IAAP), the Association of Graduate Analytical Psychologists (AGAP), and the Pittsburgh Society of Jungian Analysts (PSJA). In one form or another, Pauline has taught from pre-school through graduate school, including eleven years in the Behavioral Sciences Department of Point Park College (Pittsburgh, Pennsylvania). For a number of those years, she also held the position of Director of Psychological Counseling Services. Among other commitments, she has served as a consultant to Project 60, a Pennsylvania maximum-security prison program, and in a medical hospital setting for groups with psychosomatic illnesses. She has lectured and conducted workshops nationally and internationally, transporting Jung's magnum opus into diverse settings.

Pauline and Michelle began working together professionally in 1995. Throughout the years, they have interacted with persons of diverse professions and significant talents - persons in business, government, health care and education. It has been, and continues to be, a most rewarding vocation.

Through McKenzie Oaks Films, Ltd., Pauline Napier has authored a number of videos, including "A Journey into the Soul Shadow," "Searching for the Masculine Soul," "Active Imagination as Developed by C.G. Jung," "Ann's Log: One Woman's Experience of Active Imagination," and with Michelle "Human Strength: An Experience of Trust & The Transcendent Function." (www.mckenzieoaks.com)

"ME"

MICHELLE NAPIER-DUNNINGS believes there is much wisdom and creativity locked inside each of us. All too often our logical minds cannot unearth or translate these gifts.

Her belief emerged as an undergraduate in Psychology and Biology (Earlham College, 1979) and later as an MFA graduate student in theatre (Virginia Commonwealth University, 1983).

Early in her professional career, Michelle worked as an arts educator and professional actress (BoarsHead Theatre, Lansing, Michigan, 1984-1985 & Michigan State University's Wharton Center for Performing Arts, East Lansing, Michigan, 1985-1995). She partnered with educators interested in integrating arts experiences into the teaching of reading, writing, and arithmetic. Teachers who felt completely void of artistic talent explored non-threatening ways to experience the arts. As creativity was touched, teachers found individual strategies for integrating the arts into their established practices.

Businesses began to show great interest as Michelle raised money for these educational programs. They not only recognized the value of such programs for children and their teachers but also began to explore how innovative programs might benefit their employees and the business world. Corporate leaders discussed the growing need for creative exploration in their industries and the search for wisdom within project teams and leadership groups. Because of this feedback, Michelle decided to apply what she had learned to the corporate world. She was offered an opportunity to open a branch office in Lansing, Michigan, in 1995 for Project Innovations, Inc. and shortly after became a minority owner. She has worked with various industries since 1995, including engineering firms, telecommunications companies, start-ups, state departments, health organizations, and community service agencies.

In 2003, Michelle stepped out on her own and formed Pearl Partners LLC. Her company's mission is to help others find the energy to move toward success by creatively *tapping the wisdom within* individuals, groups, and organizations.

She is married with two "almost grown" children, and runs Pearl Partners from her office in Lansing, Michigan. (www.pearlpartners.net)

Michelle swinging in childhood backyard, 1969

Pauline relaxing after a workshop, 2004

Singing from upper alcove,
Teatro Greco, Sicily
Pauline far left
Michelle second from left

Singing on stage, Teatro Greco

Handmade labyrinth on a cork board
Pauline's birthday gift, 2002

Labyrinth in Michelle's backyard, Lansing, Michigan
Built June 7, 2003

"The Bread-Lady"
Sarah, Grandma Spamp with St. Joseph Society friends
and granddaughter, Michelle
Sarah, second from left; Michelle, far right

One Family of Elders
Sarah as a child, with her parents and siblings
Sarah is standing in front of her mother, holding her hat

APPENDIX

CARL GUSTAV JUNG: (1875-1961)
BIOGRAPHICAL SKETCH

Carl Gustav Jung was born on 26 July 1875 in Kesswil, Switzerland. When he was four years old, his father (1842-1896), who was a clergyman, took up an appointment in Klein-Huningen, near Basel. Jung's mother (1848-1923) assumed the duties required of a parson's wife during the later part of the nineteenth century. Jung spent his school years in Basel. But it was in Zurich where he began his career as a psychiatrist. He did his research on the Word Association Experiment under E. Bleuler, then director of the renowned Burgholzli Clinic in Zurich. Jung's scientific research won him a worldwide reputation. In 1904 he was awarded an honorary degree from Clark University in Massachusetts. Throughout his life Jung would receive many such honors. In 1936, Harvard University included Jung among the outstanding living scientists on whom it conferred honorary degrees. Other honors followed, including recognition from the University of Calcutta and Oxford University. He was also appointed a Fellow of the (British) Royal Society of Medicine.

In 1903, Jung married Emma Rauschenbach. She bore him four daughters and one son. His wife worked closely with him until her death in 1955. Emma Jung became an analyst in her own right. She did extensive clinical work, research, and published several books.

Jung's first meeting with Sigmund Freud occurred in Vienna in 1907. Freud and Jung had a period of lively human and scientific exchange. Jung and Freud were founding members of the International

Psychoanalytic Association (1911). Jung became the first president of the association.

Early in their relationship, Jung saw that Freud's truly remarkable discoveries could not be questioned. Jung on the other hand, as a scientific physician who was also steeped in philosophy, mythology, ethnology, and spiritualistic phenomena, doubted and questioned constantly. Jung's publication of Symbols of Transformation (C.W. Vol. 5), significantly non-Freudian, contributed to the final break of their friendship in 1913. Freud, the founder of the Psychoanalytic School, and Jung, whose school of thought is known as Analytical Psychology, are two giants in the field of personality development.

Jung traveled extensively, encountering people of many races, creeds, and colors. His experiences in European Countries, Africa, India and the United States gave him empirical knowledge of man's commonality as well as his cultural differences. "Our psychology," said Jung "takes account of the cultural as well as natural man, and accordingly its explanations must keep both points of view in mind, the spiritual and the biological." (C.W. Vol. 11) The complete man is not "Either-Or" but "And-Both." Jung's concept of conscious and unconscious, which addresses a personal and a collective aspect, is basic to an understanding of the whole personality. Among Jung's vast writing, The Development of Personality (C.W. Vol. 17), Two Essays on Analytical Psychology (C.W. Vol. 7), and Psychological Types (C.W. Vol. 6) are three volumes that most comprehensively explore his thoughts on the totality of a personality.

If man is to curb the escalating world violence, Jung claims that, "The change must begin with one individual; it might be any one of us. Nobody can afford to look around and to wait for somebody else to do what he is loath to do himself. As nobody knows what he could do, he might be bold enough to ask himself whether by any chance his unconscious might know something helpful, when there is no satisfactory conscious answer anywhere in sight." (C.W.18 par. 599)

Jung continues: "It is my conviction that the investigation of the psyche is the science of the future . . . It is, however, the science we need most. Indeed, it is becoming ever more obvious that it is not famine, not earthquakes, not microbes, not cancer but man himself who is man's greatest danger to man, for the simple reason that there is no adequate protection against psychic epidemics, which are infinitely more devastating than the worst of natural catastrophes. The supreme danger, which threatens individuals as well as whole nations, is a psychic danger . . . The greatest danger of all comes from the masses, in whom the effects of the unconscious pile up cumulatively and the reasonableness of the conscious mind is stifled." (C.W. Vol. 18 par. 1358)

Jung's psychological concepts endow the individual with meaning and purpose. He leaves us with a great task ~ a task, however, filled with hope and trust in future generations.

Jung's magnum opus continued into his ninth decade, a living witness of his theories of the importance of a person's second half of life. After a lifetime of self-examination, scientific research, and creative scholarly work, Dr. Jung died at his home in Kusnacht, 6 June 1961 in his eighty-sixth year.

CARL JUNG
AND SIGMUND FREUD ~
BASIC THEORY COMPARISONS

From our perspective there are, in this time of psychological history, two major personality theorists: Sigmund Freud and Carl Jung. The contributions that many researchers have made to enrich our knowledge of the development of personality are in some manner built upon the groundwork of Freud and Jung. While there are a number of differences in their theories pertaining to the nature of man, for our purposes these are the most relevant:

1. Freud believed that one is born tabula rasa ~ with a psychological clean slate.
   Jung proposed that man is born psychologically whole.

2. Freud saw society as the dominant agent of change in the life of an individual.
   Jung believed that the individual is the dominant agent of change in the life of a society.

3. Jung acknowledged in the psyche of man a "spiritual function."
   Freud believed that a spiritual connection was not only irrelevant but actually a barrier to growth.

4. Freud saw the unconscious as a repository of repressed personal experiences.
   Jung agreed that the unconscious included repressed personal experiences but added an autonomy of an "invisible energy" to the concept of the unconscious.

5. Jung initiated the notion that the second half of life (beginning about forty to fifty years of age) was as important for human development as the first forty or fifty years of life.

√|

Freud saw the beginning years of life as directing human behavior thereafter.

Both Freud and Jung contributed a groundbreaking understanding of human psychology.

The genius of these two giants was that they had the courage to know, along with Heraclitus (500 B.C.E.), that their life's work was based upon the fact that "I Study Myself."

BIBLIOGRAPHY

The American Heritage® Dictionary of the English Language, Fourth Edition. (2006). Dictionary.com: Houghton Mifflin Company.

Artress, Lauren. (1995). *Walking a Sacred Path: Rediscovering the Labyrinth as a Sacred Tool.* New York: Riverhead Books.

Baldwin, Christina. (1990). *Life's Companion: Journal Writing as a Spiritual Quest.* New York: Bantam Books.

Blum, David. (1998). *Appointment with the Wise Old Dog.* Video. P.O. Box 104, Medina, WA: Sarah Blum

Cook, Blanch Wiesen. (1992). *Eleanor Roosevelt Vol. I: 1884-1933.* New York: Penguin Books.

Cook, Blanch Wiesen. (1999). *Eleanor Roosevelt Vol. II: 1933-1938.* New York: Penguin Books.

Coelho, Paulo. (1993). *The Alchemist.* New York: Harper Collins.

Dictionary.com Unabridged (v 1.1). (2007). Random House, Inc.

Graham, Nancy Perry. (July & August 2006). *Staying Powell.* AARP The Magazine.

Goldberg, Natalie. (1986). *Writing Down the Bones: Freeing the Writer Within.* Boston, Massachusetts: Shambhala Publications Inc.

Hilgard, Ernest. Atkinson, Rita. Atkinson, Richard. (1979). *Introduction To Psychology.* New York: Harcourt Brace Jovanovich Inc.

Jung, Carl Gustav.
- (1964). *Civilization in Transition.* C.W. Vol. 10. Princeton, New Jersey: Bollingen Foundation.

- (1954). *The Development of Personality.* C.W. Vol. 17. Princeton, New Jersey: Princeton University Press.
- (1959). *Face to Face.* Video: BBC Interview.
- (1964). *Man and His Symbols.* New York: Dell Publishing Co.
- (1961). *Memories, Dreams, Reflections.* New York: Pantheon Books.
- (1933). *Modern Man in Search of a Soul.* Orlando, Florida: Harcourt Brace.
- (1953). *Psychological Reflections.* Princeton, New Jersey: Princeton University Press.
- (1971). *Psychological Types.* Collected Works. Volume 6. New York: Bollingen Foundation.
- (1958). *Psychology and Religion: West and East.* C.W. Vol. 11. Princeton, New Jersey: Princeton University Press.
- (1960). *The Structure and Dynamics of the Psyche.* C.W. Vol. 8. New York: Bollingen Foundation.
- (1957). *The Undiscovered Self.* Princeton, New Jersey: Princeton University Press.

Labyrinths

http://www.SpiritConnecXions.com
http://www.labyrinthsociety.org
http://www.gracecathedral.org
http://www.labyrinthonline.com/
http://labyrinth.kumu.org/vizwalk1.htm
http://www.stonecircledesign.com/menu_frameset.html

Lonegren, Sig. (2001). *Ancient Myths & Modern Uses.* New York: Sterling Publications.

Meade, Michael. (2004). *Holding the Thread of Life.* Audio. Seattle, Washington. www.mosaicvoices.org

Mendelsohn, Daniel. (2006). *The Lost.* New York: Harper Collins.

Napier, A. David. (2003). *The Age of Immunology.* Chicago and London: University of Chicago Press.

Napier, A. David. (2004). *The Righting of Passage*. Philadelphia, Pennsylvania: University of Pennsylvania Press.

Napier, Pauline S.
- (1999). *Active Imagination as Developed by C.G. Jung*. Eugene, Oregon: McKenzie Oaks Films.
- (1998). *A Journey into the Soul-Shadow*. Eugene, Oregon: McKenzie Oaks Films.
- (1999). *Ann's Log* (four-part series). Eugene, Oregon: McKenzie Oaks Films.
- (1999). *Searching for the Masculine Soul*. Eugene, Oregon: McKenzie Oaks Films.

Perlas, Nicanor. (2003). *Shaping Globalization*. Gabriola Island, British Columbia: New Society Publishers. (2000 Philippines).
- (8 December 2003). Right Livelihood Award Foundation. Stockholm, Sweden.

Peele, Stanton. (1985). *The Meaning of Addiction*. Lexington, Massachusetts: D.C. Heath.

Roosevelt, Eleanor. (1958). *On My Own: The Years Since the White House*. New York: Dell Publishing Co., Inc.

Sands, Helen Raphael. (2001). *The Healing Labyrinth: Finding Your Path to Inner Peace*. Hauppauge, New York: Barron's educational Series, Inc.

Webster's New World Dictionary of the American Language, College Edition. (1966). New York: The World Publishing Company.

West, Melissa Gayle. (2000). *Exploring the Labyrinth: A Guide for Healing and Spiritual Growth*. New York: Broadway Books.

Westbury, Virginia V. (2001). *Labyrinths: Ancient Paths of Wisdom and Peace*. Australia: Lansdowne Publishing Pty Ltd.

Native Wisdom

A Grandfather from the Cherokee Nation was talking with his grandson.

"A fight is going on inside me," he said to the boy.

"It is a terrible fight and it is between two wolves.

"One wolf is evil and ugly: He is anger, envy, war, greed, self-pity, sorrow, regret, guilt, resentment, inferiority, lies, false pride, superiority, selfishness, and arrogance.

"The other wolf is beautiful and good: He is friendly, joyful, peace, love, hope, serenity, humility, kindness, benevolence, justice, fairness, empathy, generosity, true, compassion, gratitude, and deep vision.

"This same fight is going on inside you, and inside every other human as well."

The grandson paused in deep reflection because of what his grandfather had just said. Then he finally cried out, **"Oyee! Grandfather, which wolf will win?"**

The elder Cherokee replied, **"The wolf that you feed."**

http://www.rainbowbody.net/Ongwhehonwhe/cherokee.htm